D0282464

No Longer the Property of
Hayner Public Library District

HAYNER PUBLIC LIBRARY DISTRICT
ALTON, ILLINOIS

OVERDUES 10 PER DAY, MAXIMUM FINE
COST OF ITEM
ADDITIONAL $5.00 SERVICE CHARGE
APPLIED TO
LOST OR DAMAGED ITEMS

HAYNER PLD/ALTON SQUARE

"I've done the science research to establish why stories are so powerful for human communications. Jim's book is an excellent practical guide to how to effectively use them."

—Kendall Haven, story strategist, author, and master storyteller

"Heroic brands make the customer the hero of their brand story. *StoryBranding* makes the journey easy, predictable and profitable."

—Dave Lakhani, author of *Persuasion: The Art of Getting What You Want*

"Jim uses humor and stories brilliantly to provide a road map for making your brand stand out. Everyone loves a great story—listen to his tales and let everyone love your brand. This is a book that is tough to put down."

—Sal Sredni, president and CEO of TradeStation Group

"*StoryBranding* resonates just like a great story. Like the brand-building process itself, Jim's analogy is part vision-quest, part how-to, and completely engaging. More than a book, this workbook is a must-read for those brands that want to be part of the Participation Economy."

—Lisa Colantuono, copartner, AAR Partners; adjunct advertising professor, New York Institute of Technology

"How does a brand become one seen as *the right* brand? The one about which customers feel 'My brand gets me'? It's challenging, but we know it can be done, because the best customers feel it, and even say things like 'But *my* brand is different.' *StoryBranding* is a terrific read for those who want to make this happen."

—Tom Collinger, associate dean of Integrated Marketing, Northwestern University

"If someone asked me for one book on how to build an enduring brand, I would direct them to *StoryBranding*. Jim Signorelli takes you on a step-by-step process of how to use the power of storytelling to help brands connect emotionally with their consumers."

—Larry Kelly, Clinical professor of advertising, University of Houston

"Jim Signorelli's *StoryBranding* is intriguing. To economists, advertising conveys information about a product or service. A story can help to fix an image of the product or create an association in the mind of the consumer. What better approach is therer for political advertising, where each politician has a story and, in the end, is the story?"

—Robert Brusca, PhD, chief economist, Fact and Opinion Economics

"It is almost too good to be true that this book has finally been written. Jim Signorelli blends years of wisdom with the magic of story in a format that is so accessible it makes me cry that I didn't have it twenty years ago."

—Annette Simmons, bestselling author of *Whoever Tells the Best Story Wins* and *The Story Factor*

"All marketers should read Jim's book, especially those who haven't embraced storytelling. It not only drives home the efficacy of storytelling, but also offers a road map for leveraging this tool to uniquely communicate the human essence of a brand. Thought provoking and useful book."

—Dennis Dunlap, CEO, American Marketing Association

"Jim Signorelli travels where few advertising/marketing books have gone before. He masterfully decodes brand storytelling without ever going astray from the business conversation. Therein lies his genius, as Signorelli remains grounded in a story we can all relate to: delivering a functional framework for how brands can speak truth, create culture, and transform the world. An essential must-read!"

—Michael Margolis, President, GetStoried.com, author of *Believe Me*

"We all use stories to communicate with each other—families, friends, or business associates. Jim has captured the essence of how to tell a good story that not only resonates with the listener but drives home the message in a clear and concise fashion."

—Russ Umphenour, CEO, FOCUS Brands

"*StoryBranding* stands out from the crowd of 'how to use stories' books by focusing on the structure of story itself. *StoryBranding* shows how story logic, even more than stories themselves, can illuminate the dynamic nature of the branding process. It has already changed how I will approach defining and communicating my own brand."

—Doug Lipman, storytelling coach, Storydynamics.com

Story**Branding**™

CREATING STANDOUT BRANDS
THROUGH THE POWER
OF STORY

JIM SIGNORELLI

GREENLEAF
BOOK GROUP PRESS

This publication is designed to provide accurate and authoritative information in regard to the subject matter covered. It is sold with the understanding that the publisher and author are not engaged in rendering legal, accounting, or other professional services. If legal advice or other expert assistance is required, the services of a competent professional should be sought.

Published by Greenleaf Book Group Press
Austin, Texas
www.gbgpress.com

Copyright ©2012 Ground Support-Special Media Services, Inc.

All rights reserved.

No part of this book may be reproduced, stored in a retrieval system, or transmitted by any means, electronic, mechanical, photocopying, recording, or otherwise, without written permission from the copyright holder.

Distributed by Greenleaf Book Group LLC

For ordering information or special discounts for bulk purchases, please contact Greenleaf Book Group LLC at P.O. Box 91869, Austin, TX 78709, 512.891.6100.

Design and composition by Greenleaf Book Group LLC and Alex Head
Cover design by Greenleaf Book Group LLC

Publisher's Cataloging-In-Publication Data (Prepared by The Donohue Group, Inc.)
Signorelli, Jim.
   StoryBranding : creating standout brands through the power of story / Jim Signorelli. — 1st ed.
     p. : ill. ; cm.
   ISBN: 978-1-60832-145-2
    1. Branding (Marketing) 2. Marketing—Planning. I. Title. II. Title: Story Branding
   HF5415.1255 .S54 2012
  658.8/27   2011937008

TreeNeutral®

Part of the Tree Neutral® program, which offsets the number of trees consumed in the production and printing of this book by taking proactive steps, such as planting trees in direct proportion to the number of trees used: www.treeneutral.com

Printed in the United States of America on acid-free paper

11 12 13 14 15 16   10 9 8 7 6 5 4 3 2 1

First Edition

B.821
SIG

b198798bb

Dedication

To Joan, my story's hero

One eye sees, the other eye feels.

—*Paul Klee*

Contents

PART I THE BIRTH OF A NOTION

PART II STORYBRANDING

STEP 1: COLLECTING THE BACKSTORY

STEP 2: CHARACTERIZING THE BRAND

STEP 3: CHARACTERIZING THE PROSPECT

STEP 4: CONNECTING THE CHARACTERS

STEP 5: CONFRONTING THE OBSTACLES

STEP 6: COMPLETING THE STORYBRIEF

PART III TELLING THE STORY

Acknowledgments

Like the guy who could barely run a hundred yards on his first day of marathon training, I knew I had a very long way to go when I started writing this book. At times, I let go of the belief that I could finish what I had started, troubled over how to allocate time between my family, running a company, my way-too-many diversions, and writing about something that was going to require more than just the tinge of an idea. But three years later, I finished that marathon. And the fact that I did will never be as important to me as who helped along the way. At the top of that list is Joan Cohan, my coach, critic, and creative muse. She also happens to be my loving wife. I don't think I could have ever endured what she did while reading revisions of revisions of revisions, dealing with my moody moments of writer's block, and encouraging me beyond my own internal abilities to keep going.

Then there's my management team, namely, Phillip Lanier, Pierce Hasler, Cindy Fleischer, and Lisa Edwards. They put everything I wrote to the test with difficult questions and challenging criticisms that were needed. Special thanks to Cindy Fleischer for just being Cindy Fleischer.

A huge thank-you goes to Greg King, an ESW Partners art director and the person responsible for all the cartoons throughout this book. His visual and drawing talents are surpassed only by his agreeable disposition.

Early on, and before Greenleaf came into the picture, I worked with my friend Rob Biesenbach, a stage actor and an author in his own right. Besides providing insights from his own experience, he helped make certain my subjects and verbs all agree.

At Greenleaf, I will be forever grateful to Bill Crawford for his belief in this concept above the many he could have selected for publication. His ideas and positive reinforcement were immensely helpful, as well.

I also need to thank a number of ESW Partners staffers for their enthusiastic help: Joe Przybylski, Carl Haseman, Lena Elkhatib, Joanna Worthington, Elizabeth Nelson, Ben Baxley, Sander Rosen, and Madeline Henry.

And little do they know, but the clients who kept asking, "How's the book coming?" were a constant source of needed encouragement, especially Pete Wasilevich, Terry Robinson, Neil Borkan, Terry Haseman, Fred Ward, Jim Hyatt, Don Sparks, and Michael Laffey.

Last, but far from least, one of my bigger thank-yous goes to my mother for her boundless love and support and for being, at the ripe age of eighty-eight, somebody who can still tell a good joke better than most. She will forever be my favorite storyteller.

Foreword

In 2007 I presented a workshop on story structure to science writers at NASA's Goddard Space Flight Center. After my presentation, a woman demanded, "But what am I supposed to *do*?" She taught graduate-level physics classes at the University of Maryland on stellar dynamics (the math version of the life of a star). Obviously frustrated, she said, "I want to use stories in my classes. But what do I *do* when I start my Monday evening lecture? Say, 'Once there was a cute little star named Bob'?"

I replied, "Unless you have kindergartners in your class, that's the wrong story."

She answered, "But that's what stories look like!"

We then wasted ninety minutes of workshop time because she had fallen victim to a destructive, totally erroneous idea of what a story is. Surprisingly, this happens to a large majority of the professionals I interview.

It would seem that a detailed, accurate understanding of stories should be as basic as knowing how to count to ten. Humans have always told stories, right? Stories unleash startling power and influence; stories engage; stories convince and persuade; stories are remembered and believed. How could we possibly be ignorant about this most basic form of human communication?

Not all stories are successful. Be honest—most of the stories you have heard in the last year (and even most of the ones you have told) have been boring, forgettable, and ineffective. Why is that? How can it be that we humans have relied on stories to communicate and to archive essential information, facts, histories, beliefs, and wisdom for the past 100,000 years and, yet, do a dismal job of consciously understanding and using them in the present? It begs the question: What is a story (and what is not), and how do you use story form and structure for your own purposes?

I was improvising stories in a park for my nephew and consistently noticed that people stopped to listen. It was safe to say that they wouldn't have stopped if I were reading a science report. We humans are awed, engrossed—even mesmerized—by effective stories. I was hooked. In 1980 I dropped out of the world of science to become a full-time storyteller.

I have spent the past thirty years telling, writing, and studying stories. I had to learn what works the hard way—through trial and error in front of live audiences (with far too many errors along the way). I have now performed for a total audience of over six million people and have supported my family as a storyteller for three decades.

Eventually, I figured out what worked . . . but I didn't know *why*. I began three years of intensive research to see if modern neurological, cognitive, informational, educational, and psychological sciences could fill in that missing piece. I waded through 150,000 pages of research reports from sixteen related science fields. Stitching together these individual clues, I was able to show that the brain has been evolutionarily hardwired to process incoming information through story terms and structure. The human mind is programmed from before birth to think, to understand, to make sense, and to remember through stories and story structures.

Why, then, is story such a hard concept for us to master? In large part it is because you, the teller, already know the story you're going to tell. Any wording will work for you. So we get sloppy and forget that the only thing that matters when we tell a story is not whether or not it makes sense to us, but whether or not our telling has placed vivid and accurate images and emotions into the mind and memory of our listeners. *That* takes care, effort, and guidance.

I've done the research. Now it's time to turn to the practicum: to the "What do you *do* on Monday?" That brings us to Jim Signorelli's book.

Jim's work is rooted in a solid foundation of the science of story. Equally important, it is loaded with the practical, what-do-you-*do* guidance for the process of defining, creating, and presenting an effective brand. A book like Jim's is what that UM physics professor needed.

—Kendall Haven, author of *Story Proof: The Science Behind the Startling Power of Story*

CHAPTER .5

Almost Chapter 1

If there's a book you really want to read,
but it hasn't been written yet, then you must write it.
—Toni Morrison, Nobel Prize and Pulitzer Prize–
winning American novelist, editor, and professor

My editor suggested I call what follows an introduction. If you're like me, you like reading book introductions as much as you like sitting through fifteen minutes of movie previews or listening to the waiter drone on about the fish specials when you've already decided on the porterhouse. Okay, in truth, what follows does have the requisite *what-possessed-me-to-write-this-book* prelude for those who are curious. But it also has the *you-have-to-read-this-first-to-understand-what-follows* quality of a first chapter, for those who are anxious to dive right into content. So I decided to call it what it is: a half-chapter.

I went back and forth with my editor on this. But when he argued, "There's no such thing as a half-chapter," that's all I needed to confirm that I should label it "Chapter .5." I've always had a proclivity for breaking rules. I'm not quite sure why. As a kid, I can remember hating to be told to color within the lines or to write my "S" exactly like the one the teacher had written on the chalkboard. Fortunately, my livelihood has never depended upon how well I push a crayon. As for my handwriting, many people still mistake my signature for Jim Lignorelli.

I wasn't too concerned with the consequences back then. Today, however, I own a business and have a family, a mortgage, and retirement dreams that could fill a book twice this size. It's funny how responsibility somehow forges an appreciation for rules, sometimes even rules that don't make sense. Though I'll never lose my maverick streak, I have gotten a little better at assessing its ROI.

In keeping with my tendencies, this book breaks a few rules—more, I hope, than it prescribes. These are what were handed down to us in the marketing communications business as tradition. And we've followed them for a long time, perhaps blindly. My motive for writing this book isn't to start a revolt, however. It's to recognize a more powerful and creative way to define and sell a brand's unique value.

The impetus behind this book is something that sprang out of a branding problem with a great deal of personal significance. It had to do with establishing a standout brand identity for my own company. Ironically, I own an advertising agency, the type of company that is supposed to know a great deal about branding. But we were very much like the shoemaker with shoeless kids.

Like many agencies just starting out, we weren't too selective on who we would work for or what we would work on. We were like the undiscovered garage band looking for a gig—any gig. Upon receiving a call from a prospective client, armed in full PowerPoint regalia, we would trot out whatever generalities and platitudes we thought the client would want to hear. We tried to dress up our differences, but no matter what our unique selling proposition du jour was, we knew we were merely giving bull manure a fresh aroma.

For the first few years, we were in constant debate about what we should stand for. But one fine day, as if a bolt of lightning had struck our conference room, instead of asking ourselves what we should do to stand out, we started asking another question: What is it that we stand *for*? We all had diverse backgrounds and had worked at numerous shops around the country. There had to be some unifying belief that we all subscribed to, some unique value that we appreciated. What was that?

As we told our individual stories, a voice in my head shouted, "Watch what you pray for." I started to see something I didn't want to see, both in my partners and in myself. It was a conviction that had been sitting around, too afraid to be noticed. It was a belief that a lot of advertising is hyperbolic, brag-and-boast, nobody-cares drivel (and that's the nice description). What's worse, we were card-carrying members of a club we didn't want to be part of. Hard as we tried to persuade a client not to tag his advertising with something along the lines of "The Best Damn Gizmo Since God Created Gizmos," we ended up with a wall full of god-awful gizmo ads.

"That's not what that brand should stand for," our creative director shouted as he pointed to our gizmo ad showcase. "Worse yet, we shouldn't stand for doing work like this. Not to be arrogant," he continued, "but this is everything we think is bad about advertising. Why are we doing things we don't believe in? Furthermore, when Mr. Gizmo finds out it doesn't work, he's not going to fire himself. He's going to fire us. Purely from a practical standpoint, it's lose-lose."

"But what else could we do?" someone asked. "This client currently pays a lot of bills."

Then the second bolt of lightning hit.

"Wait," I said. "Maybe the client thinks this is what he has to say, just like we think this is how we have to advertise."

This received a collective, "Huh?"

"We just told our stories," I said. "As a result, we were forced to admit our truths. Maybe we've done a lousy job of helping our clients tell their stories. If we want to create advertising that is authentic, maybe that's what we have to do."

It was a great speech, if I do say so myself. There was only one small problem: We didn't know how. After a great deal of trial and error, what ultimately evolved from this discussion was our answer and the purpose of this book. What interested me most from this experience was our impulse to rely on stories to find out more about who we were and what we believed in. Coincidentally, or maybe not so coincidentally, I had been reading a lot about stories. As if I needed more proof, what I heard in that meeting served as a prime example of how powerful stories can be.

Stories have been, and still are, the most persuasive tools in the arsenal of human communications. Why? Well, there are a lot of reasons that serve as the foundation of a process we now call StoryBranding™, and the best among them is that stories clothe truths by not getting in the way of truth. They get around our natural resistance to being sold by not pushing beliefs. Rather, they stimulate and resonate by inviting us to acknowledge beliefs that are already in place. They do this by fascinating us with identifiable characters and by inviting us to empathize with their experiences. Certainly all stories intend to sell us something. Whether it's to demonstrate the importance of love, courage, or freedom, some human value always underlies the reason stories are told. But stories reveal truth, they don't preach it.

Brands have intentions, too. But often that intention is too raw, too blatant, and too often dismissed because the profit motive is transparent. If we look beyond the need for immediate sales, we start to see something that is far more appealing than the brand's facts or opinions about why it's the best, strongest, most durable, cheapest, etc. We start to see a belief, philosophy, or cause that defines who the brand is, not just what the brand is for. And much as we form an emotional bond with story characters, we start to relate to a brand in the same way. The brand's importance goes beyond any functional advantage. When we buy a brand, in a sense we join that tribe. In turn, we invite it into our lives to reinforce who we are while telling those around us what we believe is important.

Admittedly, that's a hard concept to get when we've been trained to believe that brands should boast benefits. Certainly benefits are important. But we are humans first, consumers second. Certainly we want things that help us to do more, and/or to do it better, faster, or for less money. But above all, we are constantly striving for meaning. Brands perceived as stories to be told have a better chance of helping us find meaning than they do as products to be marketed. But to tell a brand's story authentically, we have to know it first. We have to see, hear, and feel its reality because it's there, not just because consumers tell us they want it there. What's real has to reveal itself not in what is promised, but in what is proven across every point of contact.

StoryBranding is a process designed to help us know brands the way stories help us know characters. It's a process that also helps us know a brand's prospects in ways that will foster lasting relationships, immune from any competitive claim or coupon.

There's no magic trick to the StoryBranding method. There are no four-syllable words to learn, no ivory-tower theories to embrace. It's intuitive and easily digested. It has been proven countless times to help solve marketing communications problems with solutions that more powerfully resonate shared meaning with audiences. It is easily understood because, without being fully aware, we already use it in our everyday communications. As its name implies, StoryBranding is rooted in the logic of stories, something psychologists have shown is part of our hardwiring. With awareness, we just rely on it more effectively.

We learned about this process from principles that storytellers have been using since the beginning of language to reveal fundamental truths. And upon further investigation, we found ourselves borrowing techniques from successful brands that have, maybe unknowingly, relied upon its principles.

Some may find what follows blasphemous, as it takes on a few age-old marketing myths many of us have been saddled with since the so-called disciplines of marketing were invented. But that's okay. We didn't discover the Truth. Just ours.

PART I

THE BIRTH OF A NOTION

PART 1

The Inspiration

When in doubt, don't.
—Benjamin Franklin

My name is Jim. I am a suit.

The use of the word *suit* as an epithet has a long history. I understand that it started in England during the Victorian era and was used

to describe the elite ruling class. *Suit* gained popularity here in the late 60s and early 70s as a way for the liberal youth to describe people who made up The Establishment—conservative, "my country, right or wrong" Americans in white shirts, black ties, and Nixon/Agnew stickers affixed to the chrome bumpers of their large cars. And somewhere along the line "He's a suit" also became the way to describe anyone who worked in an advertising agency's account management department (otherwise known as "those account people").

When I arrived on the agency scene, fresh out of college with a blank slate on which I expected to enthusiastically add a long series of accomplishments, I was taken aback when people called me a suit. But I had been raised a Catholic, so I was familiar with original sin. It's a guilty-before-proven-innocent kind of thing, and you have to be baptized to be cleansed of it.

So if they wanted baptism, I was going to become baptized. I did everything I could to rid myself of the suit label. I started using words such as *man* (with the dragged-out *a*), *like*, and *far out* in my every-day speech to make people wonder if I was a stoner. My appearance was half preppy, half proletariat. Sure, I had to wear a suit, but my ties looked like Walt Disney sneezed on them in living Technicolor. I grew my sideburns down to my chin. I sported the same tinted glasses that Peter Fonda wore in *Easy Rider*. But nothing worked (and I couldn't get dates, either).

Soon, however, I learned not to take it personally.

Creatives, or people in charge of writing and producing the adver-tising, believed that all account people were born with the same original sin. We were regarded as vacuous, left-brained brown-nosers who were more concerned about pleasing the client than protecting the integrity of the creative product.

Over the years, advertising agency dress codes have changed. Wear-ing suits is pretty rare for account people these days. When they do wear suits, it's a dead giveaway that they're interviewing for another job. The really obsequious among us will wear a polo shirt with the client's logo prominently displayed for all to see, but the way most account people dress is indistinguishable from how the creatives dress. Still, the negative associations with *suit* are more than clothes deep. To this day, many creatives think that account people wouldn't know good advertis-ing if it grabbed them by the hand and walked them to the cash register.

At our agency, we have a rule that a good idea is a good idea, no matter who comes up with it. Although this rule encourages coopera-tion between creatives and account people, there are no guarantees. The wounds from wars that took place long before our agency existed run pretty deep. That said, something happened at our agency to silence the traditional account vs. creative battles. For the most part, the two sides tend to get along and respect—even like—each other. There are a lot of reasons for this, some of which could be the subject of other books. But the most important one came about as the result of understanding the root of the conflict.

In most agencies it is the account person's responsibility to prepare a creative brief. It also goes by other names, such as *input document* or *assignment sheet*. Whatever it's called, it serves as the one-page summary of the creative assignment. It includes the basic background information that the writers and art directors (the creative team) will need to develop the advertising, including, among other particulars, a definition of the target prospect, the advertising's promise, and its desired effect. The account person's job is to fill out the creative brief, get it okayed by the boss, then present it to the client for approval. This briefing process can be brutal. On occasion, I have found myself spending hours huddled over the form debating minutiae with a client: whether *but* sounds too negative and should be replaced by *and*; the use of *from* versus *to*; and the age-old argument about the definition of an objective vs. a strategy.

It doesn't matter that the final brief might be no more inspiring than a blank piece of paper. Rather, priority is given to receiving that

all-important client *green light* to start the creative process. Once the brief is blessed by the client, the account person always has the six-word key to turn off all complaints from the creative team: "This is what the client wants," often preceded by "Sorry, I've been down that road with them," or "I put my ass on the line arguing the same points," and/or "I know the client is being stubborn but . . ." This goes on ad nausea.

I've always been at odds with the briefing process. On one hand, it seems necessary. Clearly writers and art directors need structure and direction. But at the same time, this practice has always seemed like an overly mechanical way to inspire originality. Consequently, creative briefs can inhibit the very thing they are designed to facilitate. In an effort to control exactly what information an ad will convey, too many planners make it hard for creativity to flourish. Additionally, creative briefs are sometimes the product of too much thinking and not enough feeling. By design, the brief is structured to require logical answers to questions that explain why the advertising is being created and what it should accomplish. Often, however, the brief will identify or label the way prospects currently feel and/or how we want them to feel about the brand being promoted. But meanings associated with feeling words are very difficult for writers, art directors, or anyone working with the brief to identify with the prospect.

If I tell you that I'm getting tired of typing right now and I need a pick-me-up, the word *tired* can mean anything from starting to fall asleep, to boredom, to being strained, exhausted, weary, drained—or it could simply mean that I'm a little less energetic than I'd like to be while I'm writing. Unless I do more than label the feeling *tired* by exacting a more complete picture of what tired feels like for me right now, you will never be able to reach a deeper level of empathy. Traditional creative briefs provide structure, but within that structure it is hard to discern the emotional texture needed to fuel an understanding of the prospect's problem.

In 1863, Abraham Lincoln was given a last-minute invitation to "make some appropriate comments" at the dedication of the new Soldiers' National Cemetery in Gettysburg, Pennsylvania. Imagine, if you will, that you were given the assignment of writing that speech for Mr. Lincoln. To help, you were given the following:

CREATIVE BRIEF:
GETTYSBURG ADDRESS

What is the problem this speech must solve?
Boost the Union's war effort and solidify
political support in Pennsylvania.

Target audience:
Fifteen- to twenty-thousand northerners gathered at the
dedication of the new Soldiers' National Cemetery in
Gettysburg, Pennsylvania, and the nation at large.

What do we want them to think?
These soldiers did not die in vain.

Support:
It is important to keep up efforts to reunite
this country and what it stands for.

How do we want them to feel?
Respectful of the men who died in the Gettysburg battle.

What do we want them to do?
Continue supporting the war and the principles
on which this country was founded.

Arguably this brief sets up goals worth achieving. But obviously, given the nature of Lincoln's Gettysburg Address, its abstract tone and dedicatory manner were derived from something much bigger than a factual checklist of what he had to say. This speech was written from Lincoln's soul as much as it was from his head. It was his heartfelt understanding of the atrocities of war that inspired the words he chose to fashion this speech. Given that we're so far removed from this time in history, it'd be difficult for anyone to write anything even close to what ultimately became one of the most significant speeches ever delivered to an American audience.

I am not suggesting that to create great advertising we have to *be* the prospect. But I am suggesting that efforts to get closer to what the prospect really thinks and feels will direct better creative output than the information-only nature of the traditional creative brief. The question is how.

As you'll soon see, we found the answer in the way stories can create vicarious experience.

ACCIDENTAL STORYISM

A few years ago, I was summoned to visit with a client's marketing team to discuss plans for a new brand campaign for a well-known bank. To protect the innocent (and myself), let's just call it the Last National Bank. I listened intently through eight hours of charts, diagrams, research summaries, and shifted paradigms. My job was to sift through all this information to find the unique selling proposition, or USP, and articulate it in a creative brief. At the conclusion of the meeting, the client asked to see the start of a creative brief the next morning. I saw this merely as a test to see if we were listening. Since I had been writing the brief in my head all day and merely needed to play back words on paper, I responded with a confident yes, without hesitation.

The next morning, as I sat in my hotel room over coffee and the dreaded thought of another eight-hour meeting, I started filling out the brief. As I was writing, I caught myself asking questions like, "Will they prefer this word over that?" or "I wonder if they'll be tripped up by the way I paraphrased their diagram," etc. As I was tying myself up in rhetorical knots, the phone rang. It was my colleague asking how long it would be before we could show them their brief. It was in that moment that everything changed.

"Let me call you right back," I said.

I suddenly realized what I was doing and why, perhaps, I deserved that "suit" epithet. *Their* brief. I was writing *their* brief, as I had so many times before, simply to win *their* approval: to assuage the client's concerns and let them know that "we get it." Not once while writing did I ask myself if my words would trigger creativity, inspire new thinking, or truly help the creative team understand the prospective buyer's problem. For instance, this brief was asking for facts about the prospect, such as

demographics, psychographics, ranked importance of features—things that could be assigned a number. And if there was anything said about the emotional state of the prospect, the description had to be stated as an explanation of how the prospect might be feeling (e.g., "the prospect is psychologically distressed, despondent, and feeling a certain level of anxiety over his lack of control"). Beyond this there was very little that would help anyone know what it was like to *be* this prospect or to help anyone empathize with his or her perspective.

I called my colleague back and said, "Give me an hour."

I quickly finished the brief as directed. But then I tried something unorthodox to see what would happen.

Instead of using descriptive language, I wrote a short memoir, delivered in the first person as if I were the prospect. As such, I described who I was and the problem I was having that needed a solution. While writing it, I became like a novelist writing a mini-story that would help readers identify with the prospect. In the end I had translated the brief into something that had more of an emotional core—something that enabled the reader to vicariously feel the way the prospect feels.

An hour later, I took both the brief and the memoir to the client. Sitting across from them at a large table, I ticked off the questions and answers in the brief and received a round of approving statements from the group. Having made it over that hurdle, I then passed out the new document I had written.

"I have something else that I want to share with you," I said, to the surprise of the rest of my team. I told the client I wasn't happy with the way I had described the prospect in the creative brief. I further told them that they needed something more than a USP.

"Huh?"

"In order to create advertising that will resonate with your prospects, I think we have to do a better job of empathizing with them," I said.

As everyone looked at me quizzically (actually, *sneeringly* is a better way to describe it), I was given the green light to read what I had written. This is the story I told:

Hi, I AM your prospect.

Ever since I've had enough money to need a bank, I've been listening to banks tell me about how much they care, how friendly they are, and how their customers are really, really happy. And I always have the same reaction: Do you actually expect me to believe that? And who cares? I sometimes wonder if there's a bank out there that knows who I am and what's most important to me.

Don't get me wrong. I don't expect the red carpet to be rolled out when I come into the bank. That's not what I mean by knowing me.

Knowing me is knowing that I expect my bank to get the basics done right. Like an easy-to-read, accurate statement. Like not being put on hold for fifteen minutes when I call in with a question. Like not penalizing me for using an ATM instead of a teller. Those are just some of the basics, the cost of doing business. And if that's all a bank is doing, then it needs to try a little harder.

Knowing me—I mean really knowing me—is understanding just how busy I am. Show me, don't tell me that you realize this. Somehow, let me know that you know I have a demanding job, a family, and a relentless to-do list and a number of other pressures I have to deal with regularly.

Knowing me is knowing that banking is not one of my biggest priorities in life. I don't have the time for a bank that is going to slow me down, so give me some new ideas that will make banking less of a chore. In fact, give me some ideas that will make my entire financial life easier.

And hear this: I don't care how big you are. I don't care how friendly you think you are. And I certainly don't care that you never sleep or that together we can make all my dreams come true.

The solution? It's simple. In fact, that's exactly what it is. MAKE BANKING SIMPLER. Stay open late once in a while, or, at the very

least, don't close the same time I leave work. Don't charge me for using an ATM. After all, you never used to charge me for using a teller. Send me statements I can understand without an MBA in finance. Don't take up my time keeping me on hold and forcing me to listen to one of your commercials, either. Stuff like that.

Oh, and one more thing: Don't just tell me you can make my life simpler. Prove it.

That's it. Thanks for listening.

When I finished, you could hear a pin drop. Eyes darted about. I thought someone might want to throw furniture at me or toss me out of the room. After a long pause, the president said, "Yeah, I hear stuff like that all the time." And that provided permission for everyone else to chime in with comments like, "I've been there myself," and "That's exactly how I feel about my electric company." Everyone was adding their own experiences to the story, building layers and enriching it with meaning. Suddenly the creative brief—that cold, heartless, analytical document— had gained a pulse.

"Where did you get this idea?" the client asked.

"From you," I fibbed. (Because, honestly, I didn't know where I got the idea. It was simply born out of my own frustration that the creative brief wasn't getting me where I needed to go.) "Isn't this what all the research said?"

"Well, yes, but it's not quite the same," came the response.

"That's precisely my point. We know what the facts are. But from the brief I wrote, the one you said was on target, did you get the same feeling?"

"Well, no, of course not, but . . ."

I kept going. "Imagine a customer walking into this room. Do you think that customer would quickly summarize how they think and feel about banking in one or two sentences? You'd hear some emotion and words we'd never put on a chart or graph. In order to connect with these people, we not only have to know what they think and feel, we also have to somehow experience what they're experiencing. We have to be able to empathize with their reality."

"Well, this is all an interesting exercise, Jim," the president said, "but what are you going to do with this? Is it actionable?"

"It's a helluva lot more actionable than this creative brief," I guessed. (Because, really, I didn't know for sure until we tried it out. But I had a strong feeling about it.) "Let me take it back to the team. We'll see you in a week."

When I got back to the agency, I called a meeting. I took everyone through the same presentation that I had given the client. And the response was immediate. Suddenly the team started connecting to the prospect. They began to deeply understand the banking customers' challenges and frustrations. Unlike what they normally got from a creative brief, this was information they could process in their gut as well as in their heads.

A week later I saw some of the most engaging creative work I had ever seen for this client.

Our team went in and showed the client how we could talk about Last National Bank in a way that would truly resonate with the kinds of people I had described in the story. The advertising didn't make empty promises about a unique selling proposition that wasn't actually unique. It didn't brag. It wasn't flowery. It didn't try too hard. Rather, it was advertising that demonstrated that this bank understood "busy." And it proved it knew the importance of simplicity.

We presented this theme: *Simplify.*

That was it. In one word, we captured the essence of what this bank was all about. It described the bank's cause. We didn't come right out and say that Last National Bank made things simple. We relied instead on inference and association with the value of simplification. This, we told our client, would become LNB's rallying cry—not just for customers who shared that value but for employees who needed to supply the proof. It's *your* story, we said. It's what you're all about. And it just so happens to be a story that your prospect wants and needs to hear—especially now, in these trying times.

The campaign was met with applause, which, for this client, was a first.

I knew we were on to something with this new "story" approach. Instinctively, it made sense. But exactly why and how it worked was something I couldn't yet articulate. I needed to know more to really apply it—before we could completely abandon the creative briefing process and make this a regular part of what we did. I knew there would be a ton of questions that I would have to answer.

What I found was something far more powerful than a new way to write a creative brief. A new approach to creative brief writing was merely one component of something much bigger. Digging deeper, I found a whole planning method that had just been waiting to be discovered since my earliest days in the business. I can't lay claim to inventing this process. It's been around for a very, very long time. It's one we use every day in the way we think, explain, or try to persuade others. Studies have now shown that this process is part of our hardwiring. It's a process that has its roots in story structure. And so, we'll call this process StoryBranding.

CHAPTER 2

Why Stories?

I felt the need to tell stories in order to understand myself.
—Manuel Puig, Argentine author

The memoir, or "mini-story," about the banking prospect I told in the last chapter won't be made into a movie anytime soon. In fact, as I later learned, it doesn't really qualify as a story, per se. It's more of a character study, or what we now call an I AM statement that will be described later in the book. But *thinking* what I had written was a story soon became one of those fortunate mistakes. It ignited a field fire that quickly turned into a blaze of research on the subject of stories, what they are, and how they work.

When I started my search, I was surprised to find that the subject of stories was a timely and popular topic. Recent blogs, articles, and websites about story principles were on the Internet. Entire shelves in bookstores were stocked with newly minted books about stories.

But why now? I wondered. Stories have been a mainstay of mankind since the beginning of language. Cavemen used them to explain

how that big woolly mammoth got away. It's a safe bet that every second of every day, somebody somewhere is telling a story. So why now is there this rapidly growing newfound appreciation of stories? It's a little like calling attention to walking, talking, or other activities that we engage in habitually.

A likely explanation for this phenomenon is given by Daniel H. Pink, the author of a number of books about our changing world of work, including *A Whole New Mind: Why Right-Brainers Will Rule the Future*. In this book he states that "the era of 'left brain' dominance, and the Information Age that it engendered, are giving way to a new world in which 'right brain' qualities—inventiveness, empathy, and meaning—predominate." Pink points out that we now have machines that do our left-brain bidding. And for this reason, right-brain skills will become increasingly more valued in the workplace. One of those skills, he says, is storytelling. Pink further suggests that storytelling will become one of the most essential skills required to excel in the twenty-first century.

Thirty years ago, a similar phenomenon was predicted by John Naisbitt in his bestseller, *Megatrends*. At the time it was written, Naisbitt forecast a growing dependence on technology. And because of this, he predicted that *high tech* would need a *high touch* counterbalance. I wonder if Naisbitt gives stock tips.

Ironically, in the case of stories, high tech is contributing to its own counterbalance. Technology is providing us with a great number of high-touch storytelling channels. Social networks like YouTube, Facebook, and Twitter are, in effect, storytelling portals. Questions such as "What's on your mind?" or "What's happening?" provide open invitations for users to tell stories about their lives. Personal blogs have become a popular vehicle through which we can share our stories with the rest of the world. There are websites such as Flickr and Picassa that allow us to tell our stories through pictures. And text messaging, as well as e-mail, has increased the opportunities to tell each other stories. Technology will no doubt continue to provide us with more tools to communicate through stories.

STORIES AND BRANDING

One of those books you can find among the others on the power of story is a book by Annette Simmons, titled *The Story Factor: Inspiration, Influence, and Persuasion Through the Art of Storyselling*. This book, besides adding to the explanation of story's newfound importance, contributed a quote that I now have framed over my desk. It simply reads: "Clothing truth in stories is a powerful way to get people to open the doors of their minds to the truth you carry."

For a marketing communications planner, this quote serves as a constant reminder of how story logic can enhance brand effectiveness. Brands can clothe truths as much as stories do. Preferring a particular brand over an alternative is a favorable vote for some truth that the selected brand represents for us. The make of car I own, the clothes I wear, right down to the toothpaste I prefer, become a reflection of me and what I value, every bit as much as the people I choose to associate with. As such, my brand associations range from casual relationships to important bonds that I might choose to evangelize on T-shirts, bumper stickers, or something as permanent as a tattoo. Certainly I wouldn't wear a baseball cap promoting my relationship with Charmin. But even something as personal as my choice of toilet paper can reinforce my self-identity in addition to providing some desired functional benefit.

StoryBranding, the subject of this book, is about drawing from the age-old logic of story structure to learn how we can better clothe brands with important truths. Like stories that resonate with something meaningful to us, successful brands also resonate with their audiences. This comes about as a result of shared truths. Brands like Harley-Davidson, Apple, Southwest Airlines, Disney, The Ritz Hotel, and many others have capitalized on this phenomenon. StoryBranding sets up the conditions for all brands to do the same.

With that said, I need to point out that StoryBranding is not about converting advertising into stories, or what is sometimes referred to as story *selling*, or using story technique to sell brands. StoryBranding is a strategic process based on the belief that story structure, or how stories are formed and why, can provide powerful lessons for brands that will help them to become more appealing. The creative technique of story selling can be tactically applied in advertising or in any endeavor to sell the brand. But suggestions that your brand advertise its history or through lots of testimonials will not be waiting for you at the finish line of this book. Furthermore, given that we are often working with seven-word billboards or fifteen-second commercials, the common story format with its beginning, middle, and end can be impractical. Rather, StoryBranding utilizes the way stories are and have always been constructed and applies it to the brand communications process. In so doing, it provides a new (but old) way to organize and simplify our thinking and to gain a better perspective on what we are really trying to accomplish across all stages of a brand's life cycle.

Because StoryBranding is rooted in story structure, it's important for us all to first share a common definition for the word *story*. Seems easy enough, doesn't it? We all know what a story is. We see, hear, and tell stories every day. But, as you'll soon see, it's not that simple.

Review

- Stories have been a mainstay of communication since the beginning of language.

- Storytelling and other right-brain skills are becoming more important as technology takes over many of our left-brain skills.

- Stories, like brands, clothe truths. Preferring a particular brand over an alternative is a favorable vote for some truth that the selected brand represents for us.

- Brand associations range from casual relationships to important bonds that we might choose to evangelize on T-shirts, bumper stickers, or something as permanent as a tattoo.

- StoryBranding is about drawing from the age-old logic of story structure to learn how we can better clothe brands with important truths.

- StoryBranding is not about how to convert advertising into stories. Rather, StoryBranding utilizes the way stories are and have always been constructed and applies it to the brand communications process.

- StoryBranding provides a new (but old) way to organize and simplify our thinking and to gain a better perspective on what we are really trying to accomplish across all stages of a brand's life cycle.

CHAPTER 3

What Is a Story?

*I find that most people know what a story
is until they sit down to write one.*
—*Flannery O'Connor, American novelist,
short-story writer, and essayist.*

Story is a fuzzy word that is used in everyday speech to describe a number of different types of communication. There's the story that is anything from a little white lie to an egregious fabrication. It could be the single-sentence dismissive, "What's her story?" We have news stories, true stories, and make-believe stories. There are the unspoken stories told by photographers and rhyming stories told by poets. Is a joke a story? A song? Is a memoir or a biography a story? How does one really know a story is a story in the truest sense of the word? Is there a "truest sense" of the word story?

ONCE UPON A DEFINITION SEARCH

While searching for the Holy Grail definition for what a story is, I counted eighty-two definitions on the Internet. Some were similar, but no two were exactly alike. No doubt there are more, since eighty-two is where I hoisted the white flag of surrender. There's the dictionary definition that a story is a connected series of happenings, fictitious or non-fictitious. If that's true, then the following would qualify as a story: *John went to the store. Then he walked into the store. Then he bought something.* Don't wait for the sequel.

Then there are the poetic definitions, such as, "Stories are nourishment for our hungry souls." But what if my soul isn't hungry? Is it still a story?

Finally there are the definitions that come with a free dose of brain pain: "Stories are narratives with a plot and characters generating emotion in narrators and audiences through a poetic elaboration of symbolic meanings." Gets you right in your undernourished soul, doesn't it?

If I buy one more book on the subject of stories, I'm going to have to take out a second mortgage to pay my Amazon bill. That said, the book that I always find near the top of a very large pile is Kendall Haven's *Story Proof: The Science Behind the Startling Power of Story*. It's the result of more than a decade of research on stories—what they are, how they work, and why they're important (the whole story, so to speak). The impetus for all this work came while Haven was conducting training workshops for NASA on the application of stories to science writing. Someone from headquarters said something like, "Using stories to do science writing? Hey, fella, that's not how science writing works." Determined to prove that there was a very real and practical application to science writing, Haven embarked on a journey to prove his point.

In this delightfully easy-to-read, *über* informative book, Haven digests his findings from more than three hundred sources on the subject of stories. Okay, it doesn't read like a suspenseful Stephen King novel, but it is entertaining in its own way as it sifts through lots of erroneous information about what stories are and aren't. And about midway through the book, after all the dust has settled around all the overly analytical, protracted, and circumlocutory definitions of story out there, Haven offers this artfully simple yet very practical thirteen-word description of story: "A narrative about a character overcoming some obstacle to achieve some important goal."

As long as we find a person, real or imagined, moving through some problem toward some goal, it's a story.

With all deference to Kendall Haven, I have one slight problem with his definition. It has to do with the idea that stories are about characters overcoming obstacles. Not every story has a happy ending. In fact, some of the best stories are those in which the obstacle is not overcome. Shakespeare called these tragedies in contrast to comedies. So with that, I offer up this slight twist on Haven's definition of story. It is the fourteen-word version that we will refer to throughout this book: "A narrative about a character *dealing* with an obstacle to achieve some important goal."

With that small fix, we're good to move forward.

A NARRATIVE ABOUT A CHARACTER DEALING WITH AN OBSTACLE TO ACHIEVE SOME IMPORTANT GOAL.

What is a good story? Haven, being the scientist that he is, is very objective in the way he describes what stories are. Consequently, he does not offer a definition of what a *good* story is. For that we have to turn to the artists. It just so happens that those artists are us. What is good to you may not be good to me. Nevertheless, there are some general principles that we apply when it comes to determining the difference between a good and bad story. As you'll soon see, these are important from a branding standpoint, as well. Imagine someone telling you this story:

> While John was driving to the concert, he heard the thump, thump, thump of his front tire going flat.
> "Oh my God," he thought. "I have a flat tire!"
> He pulled over. He fixed the tire. Lo and behold, glory hallelujah, he made it to the concert.

Although it meets all the conditions of our story definition, I think you would agree that it hardly has the makings of a best seller. There is no real reason the story is being told. If someone were to tell you this story, you might politely nod and smile. But it would be hard to resist the thought of "who cares?" Thus, just because a story meets the conditions of a story is no guarantee that it will be something of interest.

PLOT AND THEME

Throughout this book, we are going to examine story elements, but first, while helping to shed light on what can make some stories more interesting than others, it's important to understand the two most basic, elemental components: plot and theme. Both are interrelated and provide the fuel for the story engine.

Plots simply consist of the physical, provable information that make up a story—the people, places, obstacles, and efforts to overcome the obstacles that describe what happened. A plot is explained often through sequential events. And every story must have one to qualify as a story. Plots are what we'll often refer to as the *how so?* of a story.

Themes, on the other hand, are the nonphysical, subjective, internalized response to the plot. Sometimes referred to as the message, the moral, or lesson, the theme equates to the story's significance or meaning for us. If the plot is the *how so?* of the story, the theme is our answer to *what about it?* or our interpretation of why the story is important.

Plots, in and of themselves, can be interesting. I have always enjoyed the action and suspense of James Bond movies and seeing how the latest gadget helps him escape from the bad guys. But I find these movies to be more interesting than meaningful. In our household, all-plot-and-no-theme movies are viewed for escape purposes and are especially useful at the end of a hard work week, when the mass between our ears is in serious need of thought avoidance.

On the other hand, compare a Bond movie to one like *Slumdog Millionaire* or *Hurt Locker*, two Academy Award–winning films. Both have messages that are fairly provocative. The first is about the value of persistence; the second, about how war can become an addiction. These are movies that will be long remembered but not because of their plots alone. They will be remembered for the values and beliefs they evidence and how much they enlighten us. They penetrate our psyches.

Stories that use plot and theme to both interest *and* inspire us are essential components of good stories just as a product function and meaning are essential components of good brands.

Plots consist of explicit information. It's difficult, if not impossible, to know the events of a story or the attributes and benefits of a product without being told what they are. Little is left to guesswork. Plots and products are described with facts the way their respective creators choose to describe them. We cannot know without firsthand, direct experience who does what to whom in the plot or how fast, dependable, or efficient the product is.

Contrary to this, themes are interpreted information. Whereas the authors of plots can lead us to their desired conclusions about the significance of a story or what their brand stands for, we, the audience, ultimately choose meaning for ourselves. Thus, we extract and interpret a story's theme through our own interpretation of why the story is being told, as well as why it might be important. It's the lesson, the main point, the punch line, or the real reason behind the story that never gets explained.

BIG-T VS. SMALL-t TRUTH

Story themes are powered by our involvement with them. We decide for ourselves what the idea behind the story is and whether or not we agree with it. Truths that are awakened inside of us can create a loud ring. There's a name for these. We call them Big-T Truths. Big-T Truths found in stories are the next best thing to the truths we discover through vicarious experience. They arise because we identify and empathize with the characters and their actions. For a short time, we feel and think like the story's characters from the comfort of our chairs. And what we make of this experience often results in the discovery of a Big-T Truth.

We differentiate Big-T Truths from small-t truths. Rather than being the product of revelation, small-t truths are the product of description and explanation. Using the small *t* is not meant to be pejorative or to suggest that just because a truth is explained necessarily lessens its validity. But small-t truths do have less impact. Somebody else's expressed opinion is second best to an opinion we arrive at ourselves.

Sell Truth

So if Big-T Truths empower stories, why can't they empower brands? Brands and stories share similar purposes: to engage, to inspire, and to motivate. Why are we consistently bombarded with brand *theme* lines that tell us how much a given brand cares about us, how good it tastes, or how the brand will make us feel smarter, happier, and/or sexier than other brands? Small-t truths may tell audiences what needs to be told, but those truths belong to the seller. Big T-Truths, because they belong to us, do the heavy lifting when it comes to making the sale.

Legendary brand themes got that way through Big-T themes: "Just Do It," "Think Different," "Be All That You Can Be"—just to name a few. These imply basically the same ideas that their small-t counterparts would outwardly express: "We can help you do it," "Our computers are different," or "We'll help you become all that you can be." The small-t versions are tensionless by comparison. All the thinking is done for us. The Big-T versions invite subscription while reinforcing values that we can identify with.

Big Ts are found, not created.

It's important to point out that for Big-T truth to work it has to trigger some existing or latent belief. "Just Do It" won't work on people who have no interest in "Doing It." "Think Different" won't, by itself, persuade a conformist to change. In his book *All Marketers Are Liars: The Power of Telling Authentic Stories in a Low-Trust World*, Seth Godin expresses it this way: "The best stories don't teach people anything new.

Instead, the best stories agree with what the audience already believes and makes the members of the audience feel smart and secure and reminded that they were right in the first place."

Consider what happened to Oldsmobile in the early 80s. The manufacturers of Oldsmobile came to see that it wasn't as appealing to a younger demographic as much as it perhaps could or should be. New, modern appointments were introduced with an updated version of the Oldsmobile product. And the advertising theme was "This Is Not Your Father's Oldsmobile." But trying to go against the grain of meaning that many young people associated with the Oldsmobile brand led to disastrous results. This small-t truth was perceived as a Big-F Falsehood. Regardless of how outward Oldsmobile was in trying to become more youthful in the eyes of its audience, it could not change subjective expectations. The new Olds product was different, but the image and associations with the Oldsmobile brand were too strong to change. Despite their attempts to claim otherwise, it was still our father's Oldsmobile.

Emulating the way stories work is the objective of the StoryBranding process. As you'll see, there are a number of StoryBranding principles that can and will enhance your brand's appeal. The principle of Big-T Truth is probably one of the most important among them. Before introducing others and the route to getting there, let's discuss the mechanics of story.

Review

- *Story* is an oft-used word to describe a number of different types of communication.

- The working definition of a story that will be used throughout this book is "a narrative about a character dealing with an obstacle to achieve some important goal."

- The difference between a story and a good story is that the good story has a reason to be told.

- Plots are the sequential events of a story that explain the *how so?*

- Themes consist of our interpretation of a story or the *what about it?*

- Plots and products consist of explicit information.

- Themes and brands are made up of interpretive information.

- Small-t truths consist of facts and/or the author's expressed opinion.

- Big-T Truths result from our own revelations and are much more impactful than small truths.

CHAPTER 4

The Brand Story's "Cells"

Until you can almost intuitively see the difference between story structure and storytelling in a completed story, you stand little chance of being able to employ that knowledge in creating your own stories.
—*Melanie Anne Phillips, creator of StoryWeaver software*

A while back, I decided that I didn't have enough conflict in my already time-starved life, so I took up golf. I had played a lot of baseball when I was a kid. And I've been a fairly avid tennis player most of my life. So I thought, *Okay, what could be so hard?* The golf ball is smaller, and how difficult could it be to hit a ball that doesn't move?

After a couple of rounds I realized that I was spending almost as much on lost balls as I was for greens fees. One day, after letting the third foursome play through, in the sixth hour of our 18-hole round and just as my ball ricocheted off a tree to a place twenty-five yards behind where I hit it, a friend broke down, practically in tears, and yelled, "JIM! BEFORE YOU KILL SOMEBODY, WOULD YA

GET SOME LESSONS?" Actually, he added a few other words to spice up his point, but I won't go there.

My first lesson consisted of a golf pro videotaping my swing. Using some sophisticated video computer program, the pro proceeded to show me that I had a hunched stance, an exaggerated knee bend, a weak grip, crooked alignment, poor ball placement, an overly quick backswing, no weight shift, an inside-out swing plane, a *wristy* release, little balance, and no follow-through, and, as if to throw in just a little more encouragement, he told me that I needed a lot of help. I decided to get a second opinion.

The second pro conducted a similar videotaping exercise, but instead of going through all the gory details, he isolated my problem into three categories: my address, my swing, and my follow-through. (Which, of course, is pretty much everything, but he sure made it sound a lot less intimidating!) He then proceeded to spend time on each one separately. Through the course of his lessons, he got to all the same problems that the first pro identified. But by concentrating everything into three categories, he left me far less overwhelmed.

It's been awhile since I took those lessons, and I still lose a lot of golf balls. But I'm not quite the death threat I used to be on the course.

Storytelling, unlike golf, is relatively intuitive. Nobody told the cave dweller how to tell a story. I'm pretty sure Shakespeare didn't take lessons. Nevertheless, structuring a good story and, specifically, a good *brand* story is something that can be enhanced with a richer understanding of what story structure can reveal to us. And to share what I think are the most important concepts appropriate to brand planning, I've decided to follow the lead of my more successful golf instructor. Instead of throwing everything at you at once, I'm going to start by simply introducing the mechanics of the StoryBranding process before showing you how to put it to work. The latter is reserved for Part II. Finally, in Part III, I'm going to take you out on the course and demonstrate how the mechanics and the process can be applied to all brand communications, both to external audiences and the internal audience, largely made up of employees. Just bring enough balls.

THE BRAND STORY MODEL

The Brand Story Model consists of two character *cells* separated by an obstacle. Similar to the way we define a story, our StoryBranding model also consists of a character's movement through some obstacle toward some goal. In our model, the main character is the brand whose goal is to connect with or become attached to the prospect. For this to happen, we must accomplish two things. First, we must completely move the obstacles out of the way. And second, we must make certain that each cell's chemistry matches the chemistry of the other.

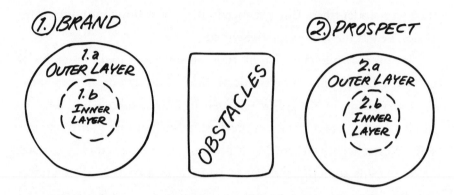

The cells are composed of outer layers or behaviors we can see, and inner layers, or values and beliefs that aren't discernible but often explain the outer-layer behaviors. Matching occurs when there is a logical consistency between the outer layers and the inner layers of both cells. In the following paragraphs I've provided summary definitions for each element of the Brand Story Model. Each element is analyzed separately as part of the StoryBranding process that is the subject of Part II. Each element will be discussed in depth in Part II, as well.

The Character Cells

There are two main characters in any brand story: the protagonist brand itself and its beneficiary, the prospect. The brand has set out to provide the prospect with more than just a unique product or service. It is looking to cultivate a relationship with the prospect, one that will establish loyalty and turn the prospect into a missionary for the brand. To do this, the brand must and deal with certain obstacles.

The Obstacles

Often, when obstacles are discussed in marketing, they refer to sales barriers. From a story perspective, we look beyond sales and consider obstacles that prevent the buyer or seller from connecting with the brand as described above. As each obstacle is overcome, the connection between the brand and the prospect becomes stronger. But until all obstacles are effectively dealt with, the prospect is vulnerable to the advances of competitive brands.

Character Cell Layers

Both the brand and the prospect cells have two layers. Their outer layers consist of physical and behavioral properties of the characters. Their inner layers are composed of deeper, often hidden beliefs and values that are linked to and responsible for character behaviors.

1a: The Brand Cell's Outer Layer

The brand cell's outer layer consists of the physical design of the product and how it functions to satisfy the prospect's outer layer needs. If the brand is a service, then the deliverables of that service, which are a function of its operations, comprise its outer layer. In effect, the brand's outer layer is both perception and reality. It manifests itself in how the brand is perceived to behave in addition to how it actually behaves.

2a: The Prospect Cell's Outer Layer

The prospect cell's outer layer first consists of the prospect's measurable traits and characteristics. These often consist of traditional demographic characteristics like age, sex, income, and education, but they can also include important and relevant roles that the character assumes (e.g., parent, student, purchaser, etc.). It might also include a life stage (e.g., married with young kids, older, retired, etc.). If you are familiar with PRIZM research available through Claritas, what is often described in one of their geodemographic clusters is material that would make up the prospect's outer layer.

The prospect's outer layer also consists of a description of the relevant problem that the prospect is trying to solve. It could be a function that the prospect wants to accomplish (e.g., a car battery that will start in the coldest weather or less manufacturing downtime). Or it can be a function that has become problematic and requires a solution different from and better than one that has been tried before.

1b: The Brand Cell's Inner Layer

The brand's inner layer is sometimes referred to as the brand's essence or its DNA. It consists of values and beliefs that the brand becomes associated with. When the brand's inner layer and the prospect's inner layer connect, potential for the strongest possible relationship ensues, much the same as when important values are shared between people.

2b: The Prospect Cell's Inner Layer

This constitutes the prospect's self and/or aspirational identity and serves as a point of inner connection with the brand. It is composed of the prospect's values and beliefs that are relevant to the brand and account for the potential strength of the brand–prospect relationship.

As you see from the description of this model, the running thread is the notion that the brand's relationship with the prospect is the all-important objective. There are a number of reasons for this, as you will see in the next chapter on the brand's goals.

Review

- Like story structure, a brand can be seen as dealing with obstacles to achieve a relationship with its prospect.

- The StoryBranding Model consists of two character cells separated by an obstacle.

- The cells are composed of outer layers or behaviors we can see, and inner layers or values and beliefs that aren't readily discernible but explain the outer-layer behaviors.

- To connect or attach the cells to each other, we must remove the obstacles. And second, we must make certain that each cell's chemistry matches the chemistry of the other.

- Matching occurs when there is a logical consistency between the outer layers and the inner layers of both cells.

CHAPTER 5

What Is a "Good" Brand Story?

People have forgotten how to tell a story. Stories don't have a middle or an end any more. They usually have a beginning that never stops beginning.
—*Steven Spielberg*

In 1898, an insurance salesman by the name of E. St. Elmo Louis created a model that you may be familiar with. For some, it still explains the goal of marketing communications. The model goes by the acronym AIDA (pronounced Aid-uh). It suggests that the seller must effect a sequence of mind-states starting with *A* for awareness; *I* for interest; *D* for desire; and *A*, again, this time for action, which should really be *P* for purchase, but Aid-pee just doesn't have the same ring.

The final goal of marketing is always action or the purchase itself. This goal is easy to love. It's measurable; it keeps shareholders happy, employees gainfully employed, and chief marketing officers from having to dust off their resumes prematurely.

However, to think that this defines the ultimate goal of brand marketing can lead to a number of problems and missed opportunities. For instance, the AIDA model ignores the fact that the prospect can be a source of repeat sales and/or referrals long after any action takes place. A brand's best customers are often the brand's best marketers. AIDA may work for a brand that is purposefully short-lived, but there aren't too many of them.

As StoryBranders believe (I don't mean us to sound like a religious cult, but this designation does happen to describe how we think) and as was discussed in the previous chapter, we see the brand's primary goal as forming a strong relationship with the prospect. Moreover, we ultimately want this relationship to be strong enough to garner repeat and/or referral business through word of mouth. It follows that, as we start to achieve this relationship, sales will naturally ensue. Additionally, the stronger the relationship and the more people the brand relates to, the better the short- *and* long-term sales outcome. In addition to this, the brand might start selling itself and require less advertising dollars.

Like E. St. Elmo Louis's model, however, the StoryBranding model holds that there is a chronology of mind states that the brand must generate within the prospect. These mind states change during the life of the brand–prospect relationship, from the beginning when it is formed and as it evolves into a bond that competitors can't penetrate. The relationship can potentially gain strength through time if certain obstacles are properly addressed along the way.

THE JOURNEY TOWARD A STRONG CONNECTION

From the time that the eyes of the prospect meet the brand, the brand–prospect relationship has begun to form. At first, the connection is weak, but over time and through the brand's activities, the relationship can be strengthened.

As you can see from this illustration of a brand's roadmap, I have identified different stops along a brand's path starting with its introduction. These connection points are like road signs along the way to Level IV, which is the final destination. Leading up to Level IV, the brand–prospect relationship strengthens as the brand achieves certain milestones prescribed by each signpost. The four connection points are labeled with what is most responsible for the strength (or lack of strength) in the brand–prospect relationship. They are product function awareness, product feature comprehension, brand acceptance, and brand affiliation. At each level, the brand–prospect connection potentially grows stronger.

When I present this idea, I use my wallet as a prop to illustrate the brand's journey. I use a wallet because it is a fairly mundane object. Unlike cars, shoes, or beer, a branded wallet is not something we usually think of when we are considering brands that can achieve strong connections with prospects. A man's wallet is a wallet is a wallet. Or is it? Using a least likely suspect helps one to see how these connection points can exist for all brands, even the ordinary ones.

Level I: Product Function Awareness

So imagine, if you will, a man who sees a TV commercial for something called a wallet. He has never seen anything like this before. Up until this point he had been wrapping his cash, credit cards, and IDs with a rubber band.

"Amazing! What will they think of next?" he thinks.

He decides to buy one.

At this level, the prospect's connection to the brand is weak. In fact, he doesn't care what the brand name is. He may not even remember the brand name. He is primarily interested in the functional benefit that the product can deliver.

Brand connection: practically nonexistent.

Level II: Product Feature Comprehension

The prospect has been using his wallet for a while. It is starting to get a little worn. So he visits the department store and notices that, since time has passed and wallets are catching on, there are now a number of wallets to choose from. He notices, for instance, that he can now own a wallet with twelve credit-card compartments instead of the four he has been forced to deal with. It's a different brand of wallet from the one he's been carrying around. But who cares? Those twelve credit-card compartments will come in handy, and the wallet branded ACME is the only one that offers this feature. He now has a connection with the ACME brand, albeit weak. It is weak because it merely represents a product function that is unique.

Brand connection: weak. Here there's more of a product connection than a brand connection.

Level III: Brand Acceptance

Two years pass and our prospect has worn out his second wallet. He decides to look for another and goes back to the same department store. By now, wallets have really become the rage. In fact, they now take up a whole section of the department store. Product differences start to become less dramatic. One brand of wallet may have twelve compartments while another has thirteen. Looking through all of the displays, our prospect sees a number of brand names he is familiar with. Any of these would be perfectly acceptable. But ACME, given his experience with the brand, is highest within his consideration set. This has nothing to do with any firm belief on the prospect's part that ACME has a far superior product or that the brand holds a strong meaning. Rather it has more to do with our prospect's familiarity with ACME.

Brand connection: moderate. Brand is acceptable more than desirable in and of itself.

Level IV: Brand Affiliation

It is here that strong connections with the brand are formed. Here the meaning that the prospect associates with the brand becomes especially important. All of a sudden our prospect starts seeing some new TV ads for IMANACE wallets. They show a picture of a handsome man who has pulled out his wallet to pay his hotel bill while standing next to a gorgeous woman. She looks over to him with adoring eyes and flirtatiously says, "Oh, excuse me, isn't that an IMANACE wallet?"

"Yes, it is," he says, smiling back at her. A conversation ensues as she rubs the fine leather.

"Yep, that's me," our prospect thinks. "Cool and confident; a real lady killer."

Now, every chance our prospect gets, he shows off his IMANACE wallet. When he attends business meetings, for instance, he takes it out of his pocket and puts it on the table for all to see. He wants everyone to know that he is that guy in the IMANACE ads. And for years, he continues to buy IMANACE wallets, even though their prices have skyrocketed and there are other wallets on the market that are just as good. Brand connection: very strong

GETTING TO LEVEL IV

I've obviously taken some license to exaggerate what happens at each connection level in this example of a wallet's journey toward brand affiliation. Nevertheless, all brands, as their product categories mature, are presented with similar opportunities for these different levels of connection with their designated prospects. I use this example to point out a few things.

First, contrary to what many believe is the case, the brand itself doesn't really start to add value to the product until it reaches the third level of connection. Up until that point, the focus is really on the product. Granted, certain product advantages may be ascribed to one brand over another. And those advantages may, in fact, be responsible for driving a favorable purchase decision. But it is important to always keep in mind that if a prospect is buying because of a product advantage, the brand name is nothing more than an identifying label. Too often marketers equate their brands with their products. But brands and products have entirely different purposes. A product provides a function. A brand provides a meaning.

The Level IV connection represents the ultimate goal of brand marketing communications. It is here that the brand starts to say something about beliefs and values that the prospect can identify with. The brand takes on a meaning beyond the product that it represents.

When there is a Level I or Level II connection between the prospect and a brand, the brand story is primarily all plot. The emphasis is on the product function more than on any meaning that could be associated with the brand. At Level III the brand starts to take on meaning, but the story theme is not fully resonant until the brand reaches Level IV. It is at this level of connection that the brand becomes valued in and of itself. Product benefits are important, but as the brand affiliation becomes even stronger they can become secondary in importance. As such, the brand's meaning adds value to the product, so much so that prospects might even pay more for the brand than alternative brands that offer similar or even better benefits. The power of the brand's meaning will protect it from competitive inroads. Additionally, prospects once affiliated with the brand become missionaries that further enhance the brand's growth through word of mouth. Is it no surprise that the purpose of the StoryBranding process is to manage the brand so that it reaches, sustains, and builds an affiliation connection with the prospect?

OBSTACLES ALONG THE WAY

The brand's journey to achieve a Level IV connection is full of pitfalls, however. Sometimes the brand must move backward before moving forward. Forgetting is the enemy of product function awareness and it is ever present. Competitive forces will mount assaults on comprehension of the brand's unique product benefits and/or confidence in the brand name itself. These assaults must be dealt with continuously. Certain safeguards against competitive threats are granted once a brand

establishes a Level IV connection with a prospect, making this level all the more important to reach. But it is rare that a brand will quickly get to Level IV without having to deal with certain obstacles. Knowing this, the smart brand will see from day one that Level IV is worth seeking. In so doing, it will prepare for its Level IV arrival by determining ahead of time what its value is. This is so that when the brand reaches Level IV, it doesn't have to backtrack or reinvent what it stands for. It merely needs to amplify a meaning that has been there all along.

Brands that have reached Level IV include Nike, The North Face®, Victoria's Secret, Disney, Southwest Airlines, and others. None of these brands just turned on their Level IV magnetism one day during their existence. As they were going through the first three levels of connection, their Level IV connection had already been envisioned and planned. Although their products received most of the attention during the first three levels of connection, vistages of their desired Level IV connection could be seen in all marketing communications. Now having arrived at Level IV, these brands are able to fully concentrate on what they stand for, which, in turn, helps them all enjoy high margins and a loyal, happiness-spreading customer base.

Whereas the connections are arrived at sequentially, each connection level receives different degrees of emphasis during the brand's life cycle. Each connection level is much like a plate that must be spun before the next can be spun. But all plates must be kept spinning, even for the brands that have successfully reached Level IV.

HOW TO MEASURE THE CONNECTION

As a starting point, a brand might want to understand where it is on the connection roadmap. This can be measured simply by determining the extent to which each level has been achieved. Measures of functional awareness, feature comprehension, brand confidence, and brand affiliation are stacked up next to each other on the following graph.

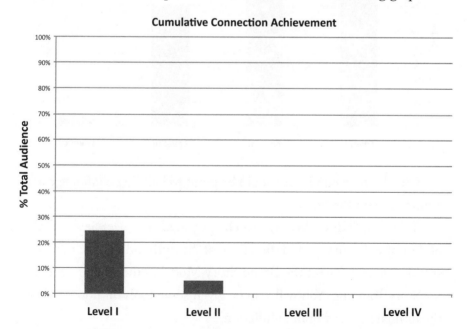

Here the brand has been recently introduced, as reflected by low-level or no-level scores across each of the four connection variables. Only 25 percent of the total audience is aware, and a mere 5 percent of the total audience has reached both Level I and Level II. Clearly, product function awareness and product feature comprehension have to be given priority.

On the other hand, the chart below shows that 90 percent of prospects are aware, and 75 percent of the total audience are both aware of and comprehend the product's benefits. Half of the total audience has satisfied the conditions for the first three levels, whereas only 5 percent has achieved all four levels.

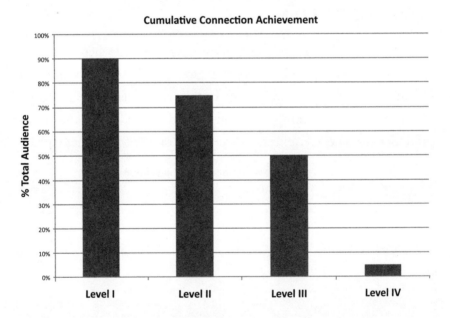

Cumulative Connection Achievement

Clearly more emphasis should be given to building confidence and affiliation with the brand.

This concludes Part I, which provided an overview of the philosophy, language, and function of StoryBranding. In the next section, we will dissect the Brand Story Model as the primary activity for StoryBranding. You will also be given some tools on how to reach the ultimate goal of brand affiliation.

Review

- The belief that sales achievement defines the ultimate goal of brand marketing can lead to a number of problems and missed opportunities.

- The primary goal for the brand should be to achieve a strong relationship with the prospect. Sales will follow.

- A strong relationship with the prospect will also help to achieve referral business through word of mouth.

- The brand's journey toward a strong relationship with the prospect consists of four levels:

  - Level I: Product Function Awareness

  - Level II: Product Feature Comprehension

  - Level III: Brand Acceptance

  - Level IV: Brand Affiliation

- Although the connection levels are arrived at sequentially, each connection level receives different degrees of emphasis during the brand's life cycle.

- Until the brand is able to achieve a Level III connection with the prospect, the connection is more product dependent than brand dependent.

- Level IV, or Brand Affiliation, represents the ultimate goal for any brand.

- The brand's journey toward a Level IV connection is full of pitfalls sometimes requiring a move backward before moving forward.

- Measuring the extent to which each level has been achieved can help determine what has yet to be accomplished.

PART II

STORYBRANDING

CHAPTER 6

The StoryBranding Process

Tell a joke that lacks classic story structure, and see if anyone laughs.
—Adam Sexton, The Writer's Store

I grew up in Detroit, Michigan. Telling people that Detroit at the time was the fourth-largest city in the United States usually prompts a snide comment or two about how old I must be to have lived there so long ago. Actually, it *was* long ago. And it's true that because of hard times Detroit has dramatically shrunk in size. Nevertheless, Detroiters among us will take pride in the fact that Detroit is a city that typifies teamwork. In Detroit, anyone and everyone affiliated with the auto industry is somehow, someway connected to everyone else who has something to do with making and selling the automobile.

One of my first jobs as a high school student was as a sweeper for a plant that manufactured piston rods. My job was to clean up the metal chips on or around the lathes. It wasn't the sexiest job, but it was important. Stray chips that could find their way into the lathes would

cause the malfunctioning of equipment, resulting in factory down-time. Finished piston rods would be sent to another factory, where they would be fit into piston housings. The piston housings would then be shipped to a place where they would be assembled into engines. The engines would be shipped to the car company's assembly plant, where they would be joined with other parts manufactured at other outlets throughout the city. Any person in every job associated with designing, manufacturing, and marketing their products (including sweepers) was highly dependent upon every other. Consequently, the vast majority of Detroit's citizenry was, and still is, brethren in one of the most important outputs of this country: the automobile. Teamwork and interdependence are values I always associate with Detroit. In effect, I have, and probably always will have, a Level IV connection with Detroit as a brand of city, despite its troubles.

The StoryBranding process is analogous to the way cars are made. It is, in effect, the assembly line for component parts of the brand story. And when the final product rolls off the assembly line, its success or failure is highly dependent on how well the parts combine to create the basis for your brand story. In this section of the book, you're going to be taken on a guided tour of the StoryBranding assembly line. This tour is designed to help you both explore and address the facets of your brand that will ultimately affect your brand's story.

THE STORYBRANDING PROCESS

The illustration on the following page outlines the Six Cs of the StoryBranding process, which we have found to be more useful than the objectives, strategy, and tactics process that is often expressed in different forms but remains the old planning standby. It shows the workflow from one planning element toward the final step, which is the creation of the StoryBrief. Completing this entire process will help you arrive at a brand communications plan that will serve as the blueprint for all brand communications, both externally and internally. The completed StoryBrief will set the stage for the execution of communications in any form and across any medium as your brand mounts an attack on identified obstacles standing in the way of a Level IV connection.

Each of the six Cs will be discussed in detail throughout this section. To set the stage, however, here is a brief description of each step that the StoryBranding process prescribes.

The StoryBranding Process

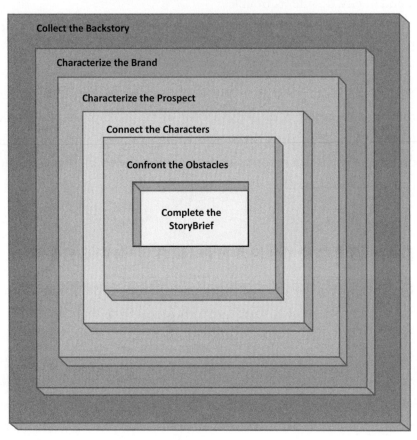

Collect the Backstory

Characterize the Brand

Characterize the Prospect

Connect the Characters

Confront the Obstacles

Complete the
StoryBrief

Step 1: Collect the Backstory

We start by digging up the backstory. In traditional marketing parlance, this is often referred to as the situation analysis. This provides the background necessary to explain the problem that marketing must solve. Every backstory is different but usually consists of any and all information relevant to the story about to be written. It identifies problems and opportunities that must be taken into consideration before the story unfolds.

Step 2: Characterize the Brand

One of the key challenges of this planning process is to match the brand persona with the prospect's to ensure a strong, brand–prospect relationship. To find the best fit, we must consider the brand and its prospect separately.

Traditional planning methods start by focusing on the prospect. For reasons you will soon learn, the StoryBranding process starts first with an investigation of the brand, with the help of management. Specifically, it starts with a thorough understanding of the brand's value and belief system and how this is supported. Is what the brand stands for being evidenced? Is there proof that what the brand wants to stand for is real and not just lip service? Most important, will prospects resist or subscribe to certain associations that the brand would like to take on?

Besides trying to understand the brand's strengths, it is equally important to understand the brand's limitations. Too often, we see brands trying to take advantage of opportunities that are far outside the realm of what is believable and consistent with consumer expectations. At other times, we see brands upholding values that their products and/or operational behaviors can't possibly support. Imagine, for example, White Castle suddenly adopting a position around healthful eating or Motel 6 trying to associate itself with the value of luxury. These are extreme examples of reaching outside the realm of the prospect's expectations. But the point is that brand identities, once formed, have certain guardrails. Go outside these guardrails, and the risk of failure increases. We will discuss examples of how some brands have set traps for themselves.

Step 3: Characterize the Prospect

Once the brand is fully explored, we then look to the prospect for insight. Specifically, we look to see what functional and emotional needs are being left unfulfilled. Then we set out to discover the extent to which any of these needs presents an opportunity for the brand in question. In story parlance, this is referred to as the dramatic issue. It consists of the problem that propels the main character's journey. That issue might be about finding redemption, love, or a life purpose. While constructing the brand story, we are similarly looking for something that would propel the prospect's movement toward a fulfilled relationship with the brand. More often than not, fulfillment results from a belief that is shared with the brand and one that the prospect feels is important to his or her identity.

Step 4: Connect the Characters

At this stage, we start to play matchmaker. Now that we understand our two characters, the brand and the prospect, we look for the fit between them. Short term, we are interested in knowing how the brand satisfies a functional need through its product features and benefits. Additionally, however, we need to know that there is something that can spark a long-term relationship, one that is founded on shared values and beliefs.

Step 5: Confront the Obstacles

Earlier, we defined *story* as a brand dealing with some obstacle to achieve a relationship with its prospect. This sets up the elements of the plot. As such, and coming into this step, we have wrestled with all of the elements except for the obstacles or those things that stand in the way of forming a strong affiliation between the brand and the prospect—a Level IV connection. In this step, we prioritize the obstacles that the brand must deal with now and as it moves toward its goal.

Step 6: Complete the StoryBrief

At this stage, we review the preceding steps for logical consistency and summarize them in the StoryBrief. Unlike the traditional creative brief, the StoryBrief outlines the entire brand story. It identifies the inner and outer layers of our two characters: the brand and the prospect. To help establish some empathy for these characters, we develop what we refer to as I AM statements for each. These take the form of the prospect memoir you were introduced to in chapter 2, written for the prospect of Last National Bank. However, in addition to writing from the standpoint of the prospect, we also write an I AM statement as if the brand were a person. This forces us to develop empathy for both characters that would otherwise be, and often is, missing in traditional creative input documents.

Additionally, we identify and prioritize the obstacles that the brand must overcome to establish a relationship with the prospect. Finally, we define the brand's unique value proposition, something that simply and succinctly summarizes the value or belief that the brand should be associated with.

Six Cs Summary

Once this process is completed, we should see a logical consistency between all of the newly defined brand story elements. Furthermore, we will have outlined and unfolded both the plot and the theme of the brand story.

Before using the StoryBranding Model, you should understand that StoryBranding is both an analytical and a creative process. Structure and sequential steps are provided to guide you across the terrain. Do not hesitate to move between the steps if you need to; just strive for logical consistency. Most important, however, is that much will depend on how creative you are in identifying with both the prospect and the brand. You'll have plenty of input to help you write the I AM statements, for instance, but how you write them will have a strong influence on how well they are understood by others involved in the creation of messages. Not to worry, I have provided a number of guidelines and examples in chapters 16 and 17. In chapter 19, I will discuss ways in which you can test yourself.

Review

....

- The StoryBranding process is, in effect, the assembly line for component parts of the brand story.

- The Six Cs of the StoryBranding process are:

    ❑ Collect the Backstory

    ❑ Characterize the Brand

    ❑ Characterize the Prospect

    ❑ Connect the Characters

    ❑ Confront the Obstacles

    ❑ Complete the StoryBrief

- Once this process is completed, there should be a logical consistency between all six Cs.

- How you write I AM statements will have a strong influence on how well both the brand and the prospect are understood by others involved in the creation of messages.

CHAPTER 7

Where are We Now and How Did We Get Here?

Every story would be another story, and unrecognizable if it took up its characters and plot and happened somewhere else.
—Eudora Welty, American author of short stories and novels

The brand's backstory describes when, where, and why the story takes place. It also identifies the reason for the story being written in the first place, as it defines the problems and opportunities for the main characters of our story: the brand hero and its beneficiary, the prospect. The backstory is often referred to in marketing circles as the situation analysis. In every sense, this description is apt. The backstory provides a snapshot of the brand's situation while analyzing how it got there.

We see the backstory as the brand's story, thus far. In piecing together the backstory, we ask, "What is the brand's current situation and how did it get that way?"

We divide the backstory into three sections: "In the beginning"; "Then what?"; and "And now."

In the beginning: Inevitably we start at the start, with the history of how the brand began, who started it, and why. What was the original vision? Does this vision remain the same today? If not, why not?

Then what?: If the brand has a history, was the brand a smashing success from the start? If not, what got in the way? How did the brand change, improve, or even degenerate into what it is today?

And now?: The *And now* section of the backstory is perhaps the most important since this is where we get handed the baton. Based on what we know about the past, if there is one, it is our job to move the brand story forward.

Typically, a standard SWOT (Strengths, Weaknesses, Opportunities, Threats) analysis will unveil important issues. Alternatively, one might complete an analysis of the brand's four Ps (product, price, place, and promotion). It is assumed that anyone reading this book is familiar with a situation analysis and the various ways it can be approached from a marketing perspective. I've opted not to rehash detailed situation

analysis checklists that are often provided in marketing textbooks. These can also be found by searching the Internet. Another suggestion is to account for the Five Forces devised by Michael E. Porter from the Harvard Business School.

Instead, and given the goal of StoryBranding to create a strong and enduring relationship with the prospect, I want to focus attention on the brand and the prospect the way an author might attend to the makeup of his or her characters.

First, while describing the backstory, and especially for service companies, we put a great deal of stock in our observations. Specifically we are interested in the culture of the company that produces the brand. In turn, we act the part of corporate anthropologists to assess the company's values, customs, and traditions. Certainly, much of the information we are interested in will come from interviews with management, but more of it comes from what we see than from what we hear.

For instance, we like to consider what the offices look like. How are people dressed? How do we characterize the people as they interact with each other? Does the company rely on formal or informal channels of communication? Is the company's tone serious or is it more laid-back? What kinds of pictures or company information are found on the walls?

Additionally, what are the company's rites and rituals? How are employees recognized, if they are? Are there any mottos or sayings that are subscribed to? What is management's assessment of its employees, and what are the employees' assessments of management? Answers to questions like these can help determine important beliefs and values that affect the way the brand is produced and marketed.

In addition to looking over the company's employee handbook, we will sometimes conduct one-on-one interviews with randomly selected employees from all departments. In these interviews we ask them to bring in pictures from magazines and/or Google searches that describe the company. In asking them to explain why particular pictures were selected, we are able to extract a great deal of hidden information about what is important to the company and its people.

We are interested in how people advance through the company and how often employees leave. What kinds of people does the company hire and who are considered *fast trackers*? Where are the power pockets within the company? Where do marketing personnel fall within the pecking order relative to operations and financial people? What is the CEO's background?

We'll sometimes ask people to use metaphors to describe their company; for example, what kind of animal, car, or celebrity does the company act like? We will also try to determine who the role models are, or who the employees see as company heroes. Language is also a signpost of the company's culture. Is there an overreliance on acronyms, metaphors, or jargon? Is the language informal or formal? What is taboo within the company? What is laudable?

In addition to observation, survey assessments can be helpful as well. A large number of standard employee assessments are available to help define a company's culture. One in particular developed by Denison Consulting, called DOCS (for Denison Organizational Cultural Survey), measures the link between organizational culture and bottom-line performance such as return on investment, sales growth, quality, innovation, and employee satisfaction. For more information go to www.Denisonconsulting.com.

THE PROSPECT

You'll also need to do some homework on the prospect. What do we know about the prospects today? In particular, are there any measures that would reflect how aware the prospect is of our product's functions and benefits and those of our competitors? How aware of or confident in our brand name is the prospect? What attitudes are held toward the various brand names competing within the same space? What is the average purchase frequency? Are there any data on differences between frequent and infrequent user dispositions? How about media behaviors?

Again, this chapter by no means is intended to provide a comprehensive list of questions that should be asked to construct the back story for either the brand or prospect. Again, there are many traditional marketing texts and Internet resources where you can find checklists if you need them. My purpose here is merely to say that some sort of audit should be conducted to ascertain information about history, the recent past, and the present. More often than not, the challenge isn't gathering information as much as it is sifting through it for relevancy.

Review

- The purpose of the backstory is to describe the brand's unique situation from its origins to where it is now.

- The *And now* section of the backstory is perhaps the most important, since this is where we get handed the baton. Based on what we know about the past, it is our job to move the brand story forward.

- To develop the backstory, we act the part of corporate anthropologists to assess the company's values, customs, and traditions.

- The backstory also helps us to understand what is known about the prospect to date. Whatever technique is employed, our main purpose is to help us determine what prospect beliefs and values are currently associated with the brand, in addition to how important those beliefs and values are to them.

CHAPTER 8

Brand First

Success means never letting the competition define you. Instead you have to define yourself based on a point of view you care deeply about.
—*Tom Chappell, Tom's of Maine*

One day, while I was attending a college introductory marketing class, the professor asked me to define "marketing concept" in front of the class. Not having been fully prepared (well, not having been at all prepared), I stood up and sheepishly answered, "Buy low?"

The next person the professor called on bounced out of his chair with a hey-dude-anyone-should-be-able-to-answer-that-one swagger. And after the professor showered him with high praise, my embarrassment morphed into humiliation. I have never forgotten the marketing concept. More than thirty years later, I can still recite it verbatim: *Firms should analyze the needs of their customers first before making decisions about how to satisfy those needs better than their competitors.* Shame is an underrated memorization aid.

The marketing concept suggests a two-step sequential ordering of how marketing is done. "Analyze the needs of customers and do this *before* making decisions on how to satisfy those needs." This was religion. The companies that followed this sequence were destined for marketing heaven. *Production-oriented* marketers, or those who reversed the order, would be banished to marketing hell. Some thirty years later, however, I've become the Martin Luther of the marketing concept.

Okay, before deciding to put the horse buggy plant into overtime, one might first want to conduct some research to see how many people will give up their cars for a less-efficient means of transportation. Even for new brands or those without an established identity, surveying consumer needs before betting on an invention makes a great deal of sense. However, for the majority of brands that fall somewhere between the relatively new and the barely staying alive, I'd strongly recommend avoiding the marketing concept.

The marketing concept comes from a one-sided notion that "the customer is king." So find out what the king needs first, then satisfy the king. As I've said, to think that marketing should be done any other way is considered blasphemous. But sin with me just for a moment. Confession is optional.

First, consider New Coke. In taste tests conducted throughout the world, the king said, "Wow, this tastes better than the old stuff. Bring it on!" But when Coke introduced it, the king got very upset. "How could Coke abandon its very rich heritage?" the king said.

Oldsmobile had a long-standing position as the upper-middle-class Cadillac. The king said, "Your car is for old people. You need to make it more youthful." So Olds reintroduced itself as "Not Your Father's Oldsmobile." Clever line. But RIP Oldsmobile.

The Gap tried to change its logo to reflect more of what the king said he wanted: a transition from classic to cool and sexy. After being

ridiculed by the king over the Internet for changing the logo, The Gap's spokesperson lamented, "[We] learned just how much energy there is around our brand, and after much thought, we've decided to go back to our iconic blue box logo." [1]

KFC discovered that the king was becoming more health conscious and was telling KFC to get with it. "You guys are selling fried chicken. That's not healthy." So KFC ran ads that said, "Hey, King, Unthink KFC. We are now emphasizing our new grilled chicken." "Great," the king said but then stopped going to KFC as often.

Whenever I give these examples of marketing mistakes, I get one or two "yeah buts." "Yeah but" they defined the king wrong, or "yeah but" they didn't ask the king the right questions. And to this, I rejoin with my own "yeah but": It doesn't matter. In all cases, the brand forgot something very important. Regardless of what the king says he wants, there's only so much change a brand can make, given who the brand is. Marketing conceptors say, Study the king first. We say, Be true to yourself first.

FIRST THINGS LAST

Writers, at least the best among them, do not start by conducting focus groups to help them decide between genres or story themes. Doris Kearns Goodwin isn't going to stop writing historical fiction and Philip Roth isn't going to start writing Harlequin novels because a reader survey says doing so would help them sell more books. Certainly, we ultimately need to understand the who, the where, and the what about prospects that will attract them to the brand. But considerations can get in the way, up front. Stephen King was once asked to comment on a story he had read.

---

1. "Gap abandons widely despised logo update," Oct. 12, 2010, www.mediabistro.com.

"No," he moaned. "It's not a very good story. Its author was too busy listening to other voices as closely as he should have to the one coming from inside."

BRAND FIRST

The StoryBranding process does what is prescribed by the marketing concept, but in reverse. Instead of beginning the planning process by focusing on customer needs, we start by looking at the brand first, from the inside out in order to discover what the brand stands for. Established brands, by definition, have meanings that are well entrenched both inside and outside their organizations. We start by understanding brand meaning internally. We start by excavating the brand's meaning from its own expert cultural historians: management and employees. And we often do this with the help of a tool you'll soon be introduced to. It is one that facilitates an articulation of the brand's meaning, which is sometimes hard to achieve with words alone. If we attempt to understand the brand by listening to consumers, this is done to help management discern if consumers understand the meaning the brand wants to convey.

The brand's story is like one of those store directories at the shopping mall. To eliminate confusion about where you are standing relative to all the other stores, there's a big X and the words *You Are Here!* Nobody knows where the brand's big X is any better than management. If there's disagreement as to where that big X is, management must align the various small X's together to mark the same spot before they communicate with the consumer.

FINDING THE BIG X

To start the excavation process, we cast the brand in the role of hero whose purpose is to save the day for the prospect. Heroes have strengths and flaws. One of our initial tasks is to realistically appraise this brand hero in human terms: what he is, what he isn't, and, based on what we find out, what he could realistically become.

Brands can't walk and talk, but like people, they manifest certain beliefs and values. Prospects form relationships with them not solely because of what the brand does or how it performs. What the brand does today is something another brand will soon be able to do if it doesn't do it already. Besides, our tendencies are to embrace novelty. As a rule, the human being is fickle and tires of the same old thing. But relationships are not things. This is why we prescribe a relationship with the prospect as the ultimate goal of our marketing efforts. Strong relationships, the permanent ones, the true friendships that we'd be at a huge loss to give up are those founded upon important shared beliefs and values. It works that way with people and brands.

While you weren't looking, value associations were being barnacled to your brand. Once those associations grab hold, they rarely let go. This needn't be a hard reality when working with a brand that is losing share and needs to change. We would argue that *change* might be too strong a word to use with established brands. The brand might need to merely emphasize different aspects of its identity. Or perhaps it needs to recast its identity in a way that is more relevant. But change? Turning lemons into lemonade is easier than turning them into Chardonnay. Furthermore, the longer you try to be something you're not, the longer you're going to miss opportunities.

Case in point is the repositioning effort that was conducted by Denny's. For years, Denny's was trying to fashion itself as a family restaurant. They spent a bundle on research, and consumers told them, "We don't think of you as a family restaurant. You're more of a diner." Denny's might have unloaded all those kiddie connect-the-dot table mats as they got back to their roots. They probably could have saved themselves a lot of lost business, not to mention a big research bill, by simply counting all the unused crayons. They've always been more of a diner than a family restaurant.

What If Who We Are Isn't Who We Should Be?

I'm often asked if X should mark the spot where the brand is or where the brand wants to be. Certainly what a brand is today doesn't have to be what it is tomorrow. However, the critical question shouldn't be about where the brand wants to be as much as about what is within the realm of realistic possibilities for change. In other words, the most important consideration should be given to knowing where the guardrails are. Just as people have limits, so do brands. Try as you might, a complete makeover of what your brand stands for presents huge risks. It is far better to know what those risks are up front than after a failure that will be difficult to reverse.

If a drastic change is needed, perhaps your brand should be renamed or you should introduce a sub-brand. This is what Toyota did when it introduced Lexus, having decided to compete in the luxury space. It's what General Electric did with Hotpoint to compete with budget appliance brands. On the other hand, it may be that brands need to be separated from their parent brand to allow for certain changes to take place. Following its bankruptcy, General Motors adopted this strategy by removing the GM Mark of Excellence from their automobiles. This allowed each make of car more individuality.

Where to Look for the Big X

The Big X will not be found in the brand's outer layer. People and brands can only be fully understood to the extent that their outer layers are revealed to us. If all we see is the brand's outer layer, then that's who the brand is for us.

Furthermore, once a brand becomes solely defined by its outer layer, its hard to see that brand any other way. Consider Xerox. Xerox associated itself with copiers. That's what it was. When it tried to introduce a computer, we resisted. Their identity as a copier manufacturer would not allow us to see them in any other way. Burger King introduced itself as the place where you can have a burger prepared your way. McDonald's has consistently been associated with the values of food, folks, and fun. Is it any wonder Burger King has never been able to catch up, once its functional selling proposition became passé? Domino's claim to fame was that it could deliver pizzas in thirty minutes, guaranteed. Ever since thirty-minute pizza deliveries have become a parity, Domino's has struggled with its identity.

On the other hand, Nike is much more than a maker of athletic equipment. It has gone much deeper by associating itself with the belief that athletic performance is a function of persistence and dedication. This belief extends to all forms of athletic gear and sportswear that carry the Nike brand. Apple isn't just a computer; it is an association with independence and elegant design that manifests itself in any number of information products. Google isn't just a search engine; it's an information force.

Whatever has been done to position the brand growing up is difficult to reverse. The most successful brands are typically those who have known and followed their "grain" from the start. Harry Truman once said, "Follow the grain in your own wood."

THERE'S BEAUTY IN EVERY BEAST

StoryBranding is based on a premise that brands should strive for authenticity. The main ingredient of authenticity is knowing *who* the brand is in addition to *what* the brand does. It requires marketers to address strengths and admit weaknesses. But ultimately it calls for leveraging the brand's strengths within the context of any change that is required.

A recent campaign by Old Spice demonstrates just how this is done. Old Spice is the Oldsmobile campaign done right. Okay, research probably said Old Spice is considered to be the aftershave that old men use. Old Spice decided not to focus on the weakness of their association with old but on the strength of their association with men and their entrenched connection with the value of masculinity.

I distinctly remember listening to my dad shave every morning as

I lay in bed waiting to use the bathroom. It got so that I could predict the exact time when I'd hear the *slap, slap, slap* of his hands to his cheeks as he would apply Old Spice aftershave. If I walked in on him, he'd put some on me, and all day I'd think I was like him. For me, Old Spice was part of a masculine ritual that would someday be mine. Old Spice capitalized on the value of manhood. But unlike Oldsmobile, which tried to modernize its outer layer, Old Spice merely contemporized its inner value. It didn't apologize for what it has always stood for. Instead Old Spice introduced the mantra, "Smell Like a Man," thereby associating itself with the core value of masculinity but in the context of the twenty-first century.

To maintain its integrity, a brand must remain true to its values. And yet, to be relevant or cool, a brand must be as dynamic as change itself. An authentic brand reconciles those two conflicting impulses, finding ways to be original within the context of its history.

Look at Abercrombie & Fitch. Its flagship store on New York's Fifth Avenue binds the company's legacy as a purveyor of outdoor paraphernalia with its role as a modern-day hangout for teens buying jeans and T-shirts. "The store combines the visual iconography of its origins—a moose head mounted over the cashier's counter, wooden canoes, and racks of ancient shotguns—with the dark lighting and amped-to-the-max soundtrack of an after-hours dance club."[2]

ART OR SCIENCE?

Most planning processes start out as science before the artists get a say. StoryBranding starts out as art before the scientists have their say. Traditional approaches that first take a look at what consumers want and need can lead a brand astray. The logic of the marketing concept

2. Bill Preen, "Who Do You Love?" *FastCompany*, May 1, 2007.

suggests, "Just find out what they want, build according to their specs, and they will come." StoryBranding is based on the premise that brands should strive for authenticity. The main ingredient of authenticity is knowing who the brand is in addition to what the brand does now while becoming fully aware of how much change is realistically possible.

Sometimes pegged as radical, in reality StoryBranding springs from a more conservative foundation. It is based on the premise that overhauling a brand's identity should not be taken lightly. Rather than throwing out the old identity, we embrace it, accept it, and figure out how to evolve it.

Review

- For new products, surveying consumer needs before betting on them makes a great deal of sense. However, for the brands that fall somewhere between the new and the barely staying alive, it's important to break away from the stranglehold that the marketing concept can potentially put on a brand.

- Storywriters, at least the best among them, do not start by conducting focus groups to help them decide between genres or story themes.

- Certainly, we ultimately need to understand who and where the most likely prospects are for the purposes of shaping and marketing the brand's stories. But those considerations can get in the way up front.

- The StoryBranding process does what is prescribed by the marketing concept but in reverse. Instead of beginning the planning process by focusing on customer needs, we start by concentrating on what the brand currently stands for.

- Especially for mature products, the traditional marketing concept can lead marketers toward positioning their brands as something they are not.

- StoryBranding is based on a premise that brands should strive for authenticity. The main ingredient of authenticity is knowing who the brand is in addition to what the brand does.

- To maintain its integrity, a brand must remain true to itself from the start.

CHAPTER 9

The Brand's Inner Layer

Once you think of a brand as a belief system, you automatically get all the things that enterprise spends billions of dollars trying to obtain: trust, relevance, vision, values, leadership.
—*Patrick Hanlon,* Primal Branding

Plan the brand story as we may, happy endings are never guaranteed. There are, of course, a number of environmental variables that sometimes spring up as unanticipated obstacles. The demise of Goldman-Sachs, September 11, or a new presidential administration can quickly wreak havoc on the best-laid plans. No matter what happens, however, we will always be in a position to mitigate risk by knowing as much as possible about our story characters, who they are, why they behave the way they do, and what can be done to help them relate to each other. In this chapter, I will discuss ways to better understand the brand from the inside out.

EXCAVATING THE BRAND'S INNER LAYER

The brand's inner layer is the existing mind or soul of the brand. It houses the brand's intention and is composed of beliefs and values it champions. Management, *not* the voice of the consumer, forms these beliefs. Once inner layer decisions are made, the voice of the consumer merely tells brand management whether its beliefs are coming through as intended.

The now clichéd notion that consumers create brands can mislead marketers to take the wrong fork in the road. —like it did for the Las Vegas Tourism Bureau (LVTB). The LVTB decided that more people would visit Vegas if it became more family friendly. So the bureau brought in the clowns, the roller coasters, large game arcades, and animal exhibits. They soon found out that Sin City was no match for Disneyland. In an effort to right the wrong, the LVTB evidently took a good look inside itself to find what it really stood for, as expressed in their famous theme line, "What happens in Vegas, stays in Vegas."

Microsoft also realized it had taken a bad turn after spending $300 million on an advertising campaign in answer to Apple's humorous comparative ads. It's as if Microsoft determined that it needed to be funny, too. "You want *funny*? We'll show you funny," said Microsoft, as they ran commercials starring Bill Gates and Jerry Seinfeld. Not only were they not Microsoft, they weren't funny.

Then there's Radio Shack, evidently responding to the need to appear friendlier. And so they gave themselves a nickname, The Shack. It's like someone you've known for the past twenty years as Poindexter asking you to now call him Bro.

These are just a few more examples of the reason why we believe that brands should always strive to better amplify what they are, without restructuring their DNA.

Contrary to what might appear a radical departure from traditional planning models, StoryBranding does not advocate a complete and total retreat from improving the way it responds to customer needs. It's just that we need to know where the line is between trying too hard and trying too much. Trying too little is arrogance. Trying too hard is disingenuous.

To present an authentic self, the brand hero can bend only so far before breaking. Time and time again we see Chicken Little forecasts by management that "we must change our identity or we're going to perish." More often than not, the only thing that needs to change is an improved sense of what hasn't changed. What hasn't changed is often found in the value system set forth by management through time. The challenge is to help management find the internalized value that continues to power the brand's engine. And it is this challenge that must be taken on first before any attempts are made to connect with the prospect. Authenticity must become a priority. What we are looking for within the brand's inner layer is not only a product or service advantage or benefit. We are looking for belief in something very important. We are looking for its cause. I am sometimes asked if the inner layer is nothing more than the brand's mission statement. Please note: A mission statement is *not* what I'm referring to. If you can remember one thing from this chapter on the brand's inner layer, remember this: A mission statement provides the purpose of the brand. The brand's unique value is what drives that purpose.

Nike's mission might be to manufacture and distribute innovative sportswear. But Nike's inner layer is fueled by the importance it places on athletic achievement.

I am not discounting the importance of a mission statement. Clearly, every company/brand should have one. But mission statements are notoriously vague, often provide little emotional traction, and are unoriginal. Case in point is this one from a very large brand: "[We] continuously strive to meet the needs of customers for total value by offering a unique package of location, price, service, and assortment." Just hope their *unique package* is more unique than their mission statement.

There are books, websites, and many consulting services that will provide advice on how to write a mission statement. Many have differing opinions of what a mission statement is or should be. My purpose is not to get into that fray as much as it is to say that mission statements are not necessarily the unique value propositions (UVPs) that were briefly discussed in chapter 3. As you will see when we start applying certain principles used to write them, UVPs are sometimes stated as a belief, e.g., "We believe in supporting the few who courageously display their individuality," or "The purpose of invention is important, but purposeful invention is critical." Sometimes the UVP is expressed as a mantra or a call to action: "Never avoid doing things the hard way when the hard way is the best way." Sometimes the UVP sounds like, and looks like, an advertising theme line, for example, "Be All That You Can Be" or "Think Different." In fact, UVPs sometimes make great theme lines. I'll be discussing both UVP statements and advertising theme lines in later chapters with examples of each. But for now, just know that a UVP sharply and authentically states the unique belief that a brand should be/can be associated with. The UVP must be real from the inside out.

BRAND FIRST IS FOR NEW BRANDS, TOO

But what about the brand that is new, the one that doesn't have any awareness yet? Should we not survey prospects first to see if the brand has any appeal whatsoever? There's a big difference between a product and a brand. Certainly it makes good business sense to determine if a new or improved product has potential. But when it comes to the brand, what it stands for, new or old, the expectations and values of management need to be accounted for first. Without knowing the beliefs that management wants associated with its brand, the brand's reason for being is nothing more than a product with a profit motive, and that will never be enough if management expects the brand to survive.

I'm a huge proponent of the profit motive. I have to be. I run a business. But the profit motive can be blinding. Without the passion that comes from a genuine belief in some principle, without the emotional charge that pushes one to make a difference, and without the faith in the difference that can honestly be made, a brand has little chance of long-term success. What a brand stands for, if not driven by the corner office, will be driven into extinction. This holds true for all brands, new or mature.

ANATOMY OF A BRAND HERO

While considering your brand's inner layer, it's helpful to think of your brand as the hero of its own story. As such it also helps to understand the gravitational pull heroes have on us. Why are we drawn to them? What is it about them that makes them so valued?

The hero of any story is the person who resolves the tension created by the story's conflict. In fairy tales, the hero might be the dragon slayer or the white knight who comes to the rescue of the damsel in distress. In literature and movies, the hero might be the person who takes action against some evil. The hero can be the main character of the story solving his or her own problem or someone who solves the problem for someone else. But either way, the hero, by resolving the story's conflict, facilitates the lesson or message of the story. Whether it's Aesop's slow but steady tortoise or Hemingway's persistent old fisherman of the sea, lessons are passed on to us through heroes. They embody values and beliefs that the author deems important enough to write about.

All heroes have attributes and capabilities that allow them to accomplish both mental and physical feats. But whether the hero can leap tall buildings in a single bound, outwit a captor, or conquer a lifelong fear, what and how the hero resolves the story's problem is not nearly as emotionally engaging as why solving the problem is important in the first place. We can perhaps aspire to the physical and mental accomplishments of heroes, but the reason we cheer them on has little to do with their abilities relative to what we believe are their motivations. We relate to heroes because we can somehow identify with the driving force behind what they are trying to accomplish. Whether it's fighting crime, beating a drug habit, or ending loneliness, our connection with the hero is not in what is being done as much as why it is being done.

Often, our connection to the hero is not something we are fully aware of. It often grabs us unconsciously. But the intensity of our connection is in direct proportion to how important a similar motivation works in our own lives. As interesting as the ability to fly through forests might be, I can't relate to Jake Sully's ability to do so in James Cameron's *Avatar*. But I can relate to Sully's need to rise above misunderstandings and his desire to bring peace to the lives of his people. Value identification, not ability identification, is at the base of any emotional connection we have with a story hero.

WHERE DO MOTIVATIONS COME FROM?

A man is what he believes.
—Anton Chekhov

Underneath every motivation is a value or a belief in some idea that is important.

Love, fun, accomplishment, belonging, justice, recognition, etc., propel us to behave the way we do. They also help us form relationships. Shared values are the foundations of governments, religions, cultures, marriages, and friendships, and oh yeah, brands. Both the intensity and number of shared values explain the importance of any relationship we have with other individuals, groups, or possessions. If our shared values are inconsequential, so is our relationship. On the other hand, shared values that are considered important serve as the basis for strong friendships, marriages, and group affiliations.

FROM STORY HERO TO BRAND HERO

It is similar with brands and how we regard or relate to them. The extent and the intensity of our emotional connection to a brand is a function of how important the value is that the brand symbolizes. This explains why some people will pay for what could amount to a lifetime's supply of Bic pens to own a Mont Blanc pen, even though both perform the same function. This explains why supermarket shoppers will pay more for branded items than their generic equivalents even though they are the same products.

When MP3 players were introduced, I purchased one made by RIO, a relatively unknown brand. I didn't care about the brand's meaning as much as I cared about the brand's function or its ability to make my music collection portable (a Level I connection). But as more MP3 players came on the market, the idea of owning one made by Apple appealed to me, and I eventually switched from my RIO. I switched despite the fact that both the RIO and the iPOD were functionally similar. For me, the values that Apple represented far outweighed any functional considerations given to any other brand of players. In fact, I paid more to own an Apple iPOD than I would have paid for a similar product made by RIO, Microsoft, Creative Labs, or any other manufacturer of MP3 players. I still would, given my Level IV connection with Apple.

Especially among business-to-business marketers, there is sometimes little or no consideration given to a brand's value association. They stall out at the Level II or III connection milestones. As I witnessed while working at an agency that specialized in business-to-business advertising, it was rare to work with clients interested in digging any deeper for the brand's meaning beyond left-brain, rational benefits like reduced downtime, quality parts, or increased ROI. B2B marketers often see their buyers as highly rational and thus spend an inordinate amount of time and money trying to outshout their competitor's benefit claims with charts, graphs, numbers, and awards.

This is not to diminish the importance for brands to prove product performance when purchase risks are high, as is often the case in B2B situations. But until computers make all the buying decisions, human beings will always buy for emotional reasons and justify their purchases for rational reasons. In the end, values such as trust, confidence, status, security, and innovation are much stronger purchase motivators, regardless of any facts that support product superiority.

Another reason why value differences are more important than functional differences is that functional differences have expiration dates. We live in a version 2.0 world. Today's features that allow the brand to boast about unique selling propositions (i.e., faster, cheaper, or longer-lasting) are tomorrow's also-rans. On the other hand, defining a brand's UVP is defining a matchless value or the Truth that the brand upholds. Once a brand puts a stake in the ground demonstrating what its ultimate Truth is, while resonating with consumers who also subscribe to or identify with that Truth, competitors cannot copy it without appearing imitative. Furthermore, once the brand's unique value proposition is established, it no longer has to depend solely on here-today-gone-tomorrow performance superiority claims. A trusted brand or one that the consumer can connect with emotionally is given strong purchase consideration, regardless of competitive claims. The stronger the connection, the stronger the guard against competitive inroads.

THE CHALLENGE TO FIND MEANING

Whether we're talking about B2B or B2C brands, both are faced with the same meaning challenge. Management teams in both environments work day in and day out with numbers and the tools of logic and analytics. Understandably, they have a hard time tapping into the inner layer where the more emotional, nonlinear, softer stuff of a brand meaning resides.

Brands, like heroes, are complex and are driven by a number of values. Finding the single value that is most *true* within an organization, the one that both consumers and employees will emotionally connect with, is one of the most difficult challenges facing any brand manufacturer or provider. Management, given its rational proclivities, needs the right tools to mirror the single most important value that distinguishes their brand against the backdrop of competitors. There are perhaps a number of ways in which this can be accomplished. But we have found one that has proven to work time and time again. It's called archetypal analysis.

Review

- The brand's inner layer is really the mind or soul of the brand. It houses the brand's intention, which is composed of beliefs and values that it champions.

- The inner layer is determined by management through an analysis of history, resources, trends, and vision, not through directions dictated by customer surveys.

- The crown of authenticity is bestowed upon the self-directed brands, those that are true to themselves, those whose actions say more than their words.

- Without knowing the beliefs that management wants associated with its brand, the brand's reason for being is nothing more than a profit motive, and that will never be enough if management expects the brand to survive.

- A unique selling proposition (UVP) sharply and authentically states the unique belief that a brand should be/can be associated with. It must be real from the inside out.

- We can perhaps aspire to the physical and mental accomplishments of heroes, but the reason we cheer them on has little to do with their abilities relative to what we believe are their motivations.

Continued

Review

- The extent and the intensity of our emotional connection to a brand is a function of how important the value is that the brand symbolizes.

- Until computers make all the buying decisions, human beings will always buy for emotional reasons and justify their purchases for rational reasons.

- One reason why value differences are more important than functional differences is that functional differences have expiration dates.

- Management, given their rational proclivities, need the right tools to mirror the single most important value that distinguishes their brand against the backdrop of competitors.

CHAPTER 10

Using Archetypal Analysis

*A brand is a metaphorical story that connects with something very deep—
a fundamental human appreciation of mythology . . . Companies that
manifest this sensibility invoke something very powerful.*
—Scott Bedbury, former head of marketing for Nike and Starbucks

It is one thing to know what the brand's inner layer consists of. It is quite another to articulate it. Following the procedure outlined in chapter 6, and before moving on to identify communication obstacles, it is important to arrive at a workable definition for the inner layer. Language is a funny thing. Words expressed provide concrete frames of reference that help us to define problems and see solutions hiding from our own awareness. In other words, we sometimes have to hear ourselves say what we mean before we can know what we mean. The act of articulating our thoughts often changes our thoughts. To help define the brand's inner layer, we use what is referred to as archetypal analysis. The goal of archetypal analysis is to give us the language, the frames of reference we need to bring the brand's meaning out of hiding.

Carl Jung, the legendary psychologist, first applied the term "archetypes" to describe universal behavioral patterns in all stories regardless of their cultural or historical period. He identified these repeating behaviors with story character descriptions and suggested that they are all found to greater or lesser degrees in all human behavior. Understanding what these archetypes are and how they influence our behavior helps us understand the values that motivate us to behave the way we do. Likewise, thinking of the brand as a person, we use archetypes to analyze a brand's inner layer, or the driving force behind why it does what it does, beyond the profit motive.

Archetypal analysis can be somewhat mystical and mysterious. The first time I raised the issue of archetypes with a client, he rolled his eyes and asked if we were going to be burning incense and conjuring spirits. But in our research on stories, I found that archetypal analysis is one of the most common forms of literary analysis. Don't worry, we're not going to go too deep into the weeds here. The subject of archetypes is vast and far beyond what we can cover in just one chapter. But we will cover enough to be practical and useful.

Wikipedia describes an archetype as "an original model of a person, ideal example, or a prototype after which others are copied, patterned, or emulated; a symbol universally recognized by all." In other words, an archetype refers to a generic version of a personality. In this sense, *mother figure* may be considered an archetype and may be identified in various characters with distinct personalities.

Archetypes are also found in us to various degrees. Each of us operates on the basis of one or more dominant archetypes. If you're interested in finding out what yours are, I recommend that you take the PMAI (Pearson-Marr Archetypal Indicator that you can self-administer by logging into www.capt.org/ppc. I took the test and found it to be very helpful in understanding myself and the way I communicate with others, but that's another story [and what a story it is]).

Using archetypes is a radical departure from traditional ways of understanding brands. But then again, StoryBranding is a radical departure from traditional brand planning approaches.

COMMON CHARACTER ARCHETYPES

Opinions differ on how many archetypes should be used for marketing purposes. One source lists more than fifty. Another, more than a hundred. Carol S. Pearson and Margaret Mark list a dozen in their book *The Hero and the Outlaw*, which is considered by many to be the seminal work on brand archetypes. Drawing from a number of sources, we have identified twelve distinct archetypes that are variations of those posited by Pearson and Mark. Each, as you will see, champions a different human value. On the following pages, each is identified in ways that can be applied to brands. To enhance readability, I've given them all a masculine gender, as in *he, him, or his*, but all archetypes are gender neutral.

BRAND ARCHETYPES

The Purist

Simply and virtuously the Purist is wholesome, exemplary, and highly ethical. He believes in being good and doing good.

Sayings a purist might live by:

"Look at everything through kindly eyes."

"Nice guys finish first."

"Do the right thing, even when no one is looking."

Champions values such as: Harmony, Peace, Optimism, Simplicity, Purity, Innocence, Honesty, Happiness, Faith

Disdains: Deception, Discord, Complication, War, Behaving in an Unacceptable Manner

Opposites: Negativity, Prejudice, Evil

For brands that: are associated with simplicity, purity, health, and good, simple living.

People: Julie Andrews, Mr. Rogers, Michael J. Fox, Princess Diana, Audrey Hepburn

Brands: Ikea, Disney, Dove, H2O, Make-A-Wish Foundation, Sesame Street, Brita Water Purifiers, Whole Foods

The Pioneer

The Pioneer is an individualist, blazing his own trail in pursuit of freedom, adventure, and new experiences that feed his soul. Whether gearing up to climb Mount Everest or going off in a Jeep Wrangler, the Pioneer looks for brands that allow him to experience life to the fullest. The Pioneer is usually an early adopter of invention.

Sayings a pioneer might live by:

"I'll sleep when I'm dead."

"The journey is more important than the destination."

"Because it's there."

Champions values such as: Exploration, Freedom, Adventure, Independence, Experimentation, Self-reliance, Ambition, Challenge, Bravery, Confidence

Disdains: Boundaries, Boredom, Limitations, Stagnation

Opposites: Conformity, Avoidance, Complacency

For brands that: foster discovery.

People: Amelia Earhart, Christopher Columbus, Neil Armstrong, Billy Jean King, Stephen Hawking

Brands: Groupon, Trader Joe's, North Face, Jeep, The Discovery Channel

The Source

The Source is looked upon as the all-knowing provider of knowledge. He devours information in the pursuit of knowledge and expertise. He has a high level of curiosity and is looked to for advice and opinions.

Sayings a source might live by:

"We owe it to ourselves to find the truth."

"Knowledge is power."

Champions values such as: Truth, Knowledge, Expertise, Intelligence, Rigor, Diligence, Objectivity, Commitment, Depth, Education, Discipline, Clarity

Disdains: Uncertainty, Deception, Falsehood

Opposites: Irrationality, Naiveté, Dishonesty, Ignorance, Impetuousness, Treachery, Bias

For brands that: are looked upon for trusted advice, knowledge, or specialized expertise.

People: Oprah Winfrey, Dr. Phil, Albert Einstein

Brands: Harvard, Bloomberg, McKinsey, Forrester, *Wall Street Journal*

The Conqueror

The Conqueror is noble and is identified by an ability to meet and overcome adversity. He is steadfast when meeting challenges head on, no matter how difficult. He is relentless, resilient, and confident in his abilities and feels that anything he earns is well deserved.

Sayings a conqueror might live by:

"Winning is everything."

"Winning takes talent, to repeat takes character."

Champions values such as: Courage, Determination, Endurance, Persistence, Success, Elitism, Strength, Status, Honor

Disdains: Weakness, Self-Doubt, Defeat, Vulnerability

Opposites: Fearfulness, Selfishness, Cowardice, Failure, Pessimism, Giving Up

For brands that: challenge, inspire, and empower peak performance.

People: Vince Lombardi, Lance Armstrong, Michael Jordan

Brands: The Marines, Nike, Weight Watchers, Gatorade

The Rebel

The Rebel is unsatisfied with the status quo and abhors convention. His behavior may be disruptive or even shocking and outrageous to some, but to others he represents someone who will do whatever it takes to protect his self-expression.

Sayings a rebel might live by:

"Born free."

"Rules are meant to be broken."

"Take the road less traveled."

Champions values such as: Freedom, Nonconformity, Independence, Individuality, Controversy, Rebellion, Daringness, Boldness, Defiance

Disdains: Powerlessness, Loss of identity

Opposites: Group-think, Dependence, Conformity, Passiveness, Timidity, Cowardice

For brands that: rebel against convention, take chances, and pride themselves on their individuality.

People: Howard Stern, Dennis Rodman, Quentin Tarantino, Lady GaGa, James Dean

Brands: Harley-Davidson, Red Bull, GoDaddy, Converse, Xgames, World Wrestling Federation (WWF)

The Wizard

The Wizard seeks out experiences that transform the ordinary into the extraordinary. He represents the universal message of mystery, thrill, and novelty. The Wizard seeks experiences that make his dreams come true, whether it's the wonder of technology that never quits, magical potions that fight the effects of aging, or a golden passport to all the world has to offer.

Sayings a wizard might live by:

"Anything is possible."

"Dreams do come true."

"Wonders never cease."

Champions values such as: Magic, Imagination, Joy, Curiosity, Optimism, Fun, Surprise

Disdains: Ordinariness, Failure, Status Quo, Ineffectiveness

Opposites: Boredom, Same ole same ole, Pessimism, Lifelessness, Negativity

For brands that: transform and create miracles.

People: Steven Spielberg, George Lucas, Harry Potter, Billy Mays, The Wizard of Oz, Steve Jobs

Brands: Pixar, Lotto, Viagra, Cirque du Soleil, Disney World, Apple

The Straight Shooter

The Straight Shooter abhors pretension and is no-nonsense. He will say it like it is and behave in ways he believes are true to himself. He values *being real* in all that he does and in his relationships with others. He's friendly and informal. He's not one to keep up with the Joneses and marches to the beat of his own voice.

Sayings a straight shooter might live by:

"I am who I am."

"Be true to yourself."

"Tell it like it is."

Champions values such as: Realism, Authenticity, Honesty, Modesty, Frankness

Disdains: Faking it, Self-delusion, Deceit

Opposites: Pretension, Superficiality, Arrogance,

For brands that: are common and everyday. They tell it like it is and promote function over form or style.

People: Andre Agassi, Simon Cowell, Whoopi Goldberg, Charles Barkley

Brands: Levi's, Miller Beer, Southwest Airlines, Wrangler Jeans, Jim Beam

The Seducer

The Seducer unsurprisingly desires romance, intimacy, and sensual pleasure. He's not afraid to indulge and especially enjoys products and brands that hold strong sex appeal and that promise to boost attractiveness and desirability.

Sayings a seducer might live by:

"Love conquers all."

"All you need is love."

"A little romance goes a long way."

Champions values such as: Love, Sensuality, Affection, Intimacy, Beauty, Passion, Desire, Ecstasy, Connection, Enjoyment, Pleasure

Disdains: Solitude, Unattractiveness, Plainness

Opposites: Hate, Brute Force, Purity

For brands that: provide a sense of romance, connection, and sensual enjoyment.

People: Marilyn Monroe, Hugh Hefner, Bo Derek, Scarlett Johannson

Brands: Victoria's Secret, Godiva, DeBeers, Courvoisier, Axe, 1-800-FLOWERS.COM

The Entertainer

The Entertainer is your typical clown or prankster—a fun-loving free spirit who wants only to live in the moment and have a good time doing it. He has a unique ability to capture and transfix an audience's attention. He enjoys brands that employ humor and promise fun times.

Sayings an entertainer might live by:

"Laughter is the best medicine."

"The most wasted of all days is one without laughter."

"A man isn't poor if he can still laugh."

Champions values such as: Humor, Spontaneity, Charm, Youthfulness, Laughter, Gregariousness, Levity, Happiness, Fun

Disdains: Seriousness, Gravity, Tragedy, Depression, Boredom

Opposites: Stoicism, Puritanism, Humorlessness, Sadness

For brands that: help customers enjoy themselves through fun and humor.

People: Jerry Lewis, Robin Williams, Steve Martin, Jerry Seinfeld, Jim Carrey

Brands: Bazooka Bubble Gum, Dr. Pepper, Jack in the Box, Looney Tunes, Doritos, M&M's, Comedy Central, Snickers, Bud Light

The Protector

The Protector values compassion and generosity. He puts others first, providing tender loving care, support, and reassurance.

Sayings a protector might live by:

"Love Thy Neighbor."

"Take Care of Yourself."

"Lead by Compassion."

Champions values such as: Compassion, Motherly Advice, Hospitality, Protection, Comfort, Empathy, Generosity, Thoughtfulness, Sincerity, Sharing, Warmth, Wisdom

Disdains: Cruelty, Hatred, Bitterness, Harshness

Opposites: Selfishness, Carelessness

For brands that: are caring and nurturing, providing comfort and peace of mind when customers especially need it.

People: Florence Henderson, Mother Teresa, Andy Griffith, Florence Nightingale

Brands: Gerber, Cracker Barrel, Campbell's Soup, Allstate, Johnson & Johnson, Kraft

The Imagineer

The Imagineer is an artist, an innovator, and a dreamer. He summons artistry and imagination to express himself and his vision of the world.

Sayings an imagineer might live by:

"Imagination is possibility."

"What you believe can be conceived."

"Life is but a dream."

Champions values such as: Creativity, Passion, Ingenuity, Vision, Creation, Innovation, Originality, Imagination, Uniqueness, Artistry, Independent Thinking

Disdains: Constraining Order, Structure, Boredom, Sameness, The Expected, Limitations, Directives

Opposites: Traditionalist, Follower, Literalist, Fundamentalist

For brands that: enable their customers to create.

People: John Lennon, Pablo Picasso, Michael Jackson, George Orwell

Brands: Lego, YouTube, iPad, Crayola, Nikon, Paper Source, Photoshop, 3M

The Emperor

The Emperor is the boss, the chief, king of the castle, the *capo di tutti capi*. He exudes power and exerts leadership and dominance over others. He prefers products that offer an opportunity to stand above the crowd, whether in price, quality, service, or performance.

Sayings an emperor might live by:

"It's good to be king."

"Rise above the crowd."

"Being number one is its own reward."

Champions values such as: Leadership, Strength, Determination, Influence, Respect, Dominance, Prosperity, Confidence, Control, Wealth

Disdains: Losing, Chaos, Being Poor, Lowliness, Shoddiness

Opposites: Following, Laziness, Powerlessness, Subservience, Weakness, Submissiveness, Inconsequence

For brands that: denote power and help build customers' leadership and superiority.

People: Bill Gates, Donald Trump, Michael Bloomberg, Warren Buffett, Mark Zuckerberg, Margaret Thatcher, Hillary Clinton

Brands: Porsche, The Peninsula, American Express, Cartier, Chanel, John Walker Blue, The Robb Report, Rolex, Tiffany, The Four Seasons, Cadillac

APPLYING ARCHETYPES

Using archetypes to describe the character of the brand story is an extremely helpful way to start articulating motivations, perceptions, likes, dislikes, and a whole host of psychological traits that explain behavior. In that way, we become immersed in the brand as a person, the hero of our story.

Our process for arriving at archetypes differs from what is prescribed by the Mark/Pearson model. We do not adhere to the same strict guidelines that require a selection of one and only one archetype that represents the brand. We do, however, wholeheartedly support their notion that it is important to characterize a brand in a simple, easy-to-comprehend, memorable way. And we are well aware of studies that have been conducted showing how blending or compromising archetypes adds to brand identity confusion. However, we believe that a rigid adherence to this or any given list of archetypes, no matter how well researched, will limit one's ability to find inner-layer uniqueness vs. competing brands.

From the twelve archetypes above, we divide them into two piles. The first pile consists of what we are or could be. The second pile consists of archetypes that are way outside the realm of possibilities. At this stage in developing the brand story, it is too premature to land on an archetypal description of the brand. It is more advisable to wait until Step 3, characterizing the prospect, for that.

With that said, however, I need to point out an important caveat with archetypal analysis. Our main objective in using archetypes is to provide a useful frame of reference when referring to brand values and beliefs. Our objective is not, I repeat NOT, to arrive at a rigid archetypal description of the brand from the twelve archetypes that we have chosen to use. Archetypes should be used as an aid to judgment.

Striving to become as single-minded as possible is necessary. However, deciding on one archetype as described in our definitions of that archetype can lead to big mistakes. It is important to allow for flexibility, understanding that there are variations and nuances to each archetype described. Furthermore, archetypes can blend into each other; their borders are not firm and impenetrable. It is better to think of a brand as LIKE a hero, and/or LIKE a magician, than to decide whether or not there is a hand-in-glove fit between a given brand and a particular archetype. It is perfectly okay (and we've done it ourselves on many occasions) to invent an archetypal description that is not included in the twelve we have described. Again, avoid seeing these twelve archetypes as hard-and-fast brand descriptors. Rather, see them as providing guidelines that will, if allowed, enhance productive and insightful discussions about the brand's inner layer. Archetypal analysis is a means to an end and not an end in itself.

FINAL THOUGHTS ON YOUR BRAND'S INNER LAYER

One of the most important acknowledgments we make using the StoryBranding process is that brands are more complex than what they appear to be on the surface, which is often limited to advantage and benefit descriptions. I'm often asked if the brand's inner layer is the same as the brand's *personality* or *essence*. Those two terms mean different things to different people, so I can't compare and contrast. Regardless of what it's compared to, the brand's inner layer, stripped down to its core and plainly stated, is the body of values and beliefs that a brand stands for and is associated with. To achieve a Level IV connection with the prospect, shared brand–prospect values must come into play, the same way shared values define our closest relationships with people.

Archetypal analysis is a diagnostic tool for the purpose of aiding judgment. It is not an exact science and does not purport to be. Its main purpose is to provide a common language that helps us relate to the brand as a person. By studying, comparing, and contrasting brands in this way, it is much easier to identify a brand's value system.

If you're interested in reading more about archetypes and how they are applied to branding, I recommend *Literature and Film as Modern Mythology* by William K. Ferrell.

Review

- The goal of archetypal analysis is to give us the language, the frames of reference, that we need to bring the brand's meaning out of hiding.

- Thinking of the brand as a person, we use archetypes to analyze a brand's inner layer, or the driving force behind why it does what it does, beyond the profit motive.

- Wikipedia describes an archetype as "an original model of a person, ideal example, or a prototype after which others are copied, patterned, or emulated; a symbol universally recognized by all."

- If an archetype is to be invented from a combination or blending of different archetypes, it needs to be described in not more than two words, e.g., the *creative-maverick* or the *hero-joker*.

- Archetypal analysis is a means to an end and not an end in itself.

CHAPTER 11

The Brand's Outer Layer

Companies have to wake up to the fact that they are more
than a product on a shelf. They're behavior as well.
—Robert Haas, Levi Strauss

The brand's inner and outer layers are akin to themes and plots in stories. Story themes, like the brand's inner layer, consist of a deeper purpose. Themes provide the means through which the author or the brand supply meaning. The plot, like the brand's outer layer, explains the *how*. For stories, plots tell how the character deals with certain obstacles to achieve some goal. For brands, the outer layer explains how a brand's features and benefits help the prospect deal with certain obstacles to achieve some goal.

A constant debate among story writers is whether to start with the plot or the theme. The *plotters* believe that one should just start with the plot and see where things go. According to them, the theme will just naturally reveal itself. The *themers*, on the other hand, believe that one should identify the purpose of the story first and build the plot around it. This is to make certain that intention never gets lost. Either way, there needs to be a balance between plot and theme. A great plot with an insignificant message is mere entertainment and probably soon forgotten. A great message with a boring plot may never get the attention it needs to resonate.

But one has to start somewhere. And when it comes to developing brand stories, we subscribe to the *themers'* point of view. As we've suggested earlier, this is because we believe that, when all is said and done, the brand's inner layer is ultimately more important to achieving a Level IV connection. The brand's outer layer or how it solves a certain problem will be copied or outdone by some innovation someday. On the other hand, the brand's inner layer, or what it stands for and represents, can last forever. And since inner layers are emotionally charged, they are more responsible for the brand's overall magnetism.

While analyzing the brand's inner layer, you've no doubt discovered a number of different themes that your brand can readily associate with. We are not at the stage where it is important to consider *how* these values and beliefs would manifest themselves through product features and benefits. If your brand is The Imagineer, how does that get revealed? If you are The Protector, then how do the brand's features and benefits serve as proof? Contary to what is often prescribed, we believe that the outer layer's purpose is to serve the inner layer, not vice versa. Certainly the purpose of the outer layer is to show the prospect how the brand can solve problems. But a more important purpose, we believe, is to support or validate the brand's meaning.

For instance, The Ritz Hotel can be described by The King archetype. It has long been known for being the hotel where "ladies and gentlemen serve ladies and gentlemen." The values of success and elitism are celebrated there. The theme of their story stems from the belief that accomplished people deserve service that goes beyond the ordinary. How does this manifest itself? That's where the brand's outer layer goes to work. The Ritz demonstrates this belief by employing four people for every guest, by allowing employees to spend up to $2,000 a year to satisfy a single guest, and by making sure that, from the moment you pull up your car until the time you leave, you are treated like a rock star. These features and benefits explain the Ritz's *how so?*

We often see marketers getting their inner layer (theme) mixed up with their outer layer (plot). Actually, this problem is quite prevalent. When we first interview new or prospective clients, one of the first questions we ask is, "What makes your brand significant?" This is often referred to as an "elevator pitch". Invariably, we get an answer that is the domain of the outer layer, e.g., "Our restaurants specialize in providing food with unique tastes and textures" or "We're the biggest network of health clubs in the United States" or "Our casinos have the loosest slots."

Marketers often refer to their specialness in very concrete, rational terms. Describing the brand this way is like describing its body, without regard for its soul. One of the reasons why the question of uniqueness is relegated to the brand's outer layer has to do with our training. Since the days of Rosser Reeves, once considered the father of modern advertising, marketers have been taught to describe brand differences functionally and rationally in terms of what Reeves described as a brand's unique selling proposition or USP. Unfortunately, this is usually linked to something the brand does as opposed to what it means. And, as we discussed in the last chapter, the hero's behavior is not nearly as important as his or her motivation.

After years of asking clients to tell us about their USPs or give us their elevator pitches, I came to the realization that most of them stink. But then, I also came to the realization that my question stinks as well. If one is looking for a description of the inner layer, this is not the way to get it. The inner layer can be pretty squishy and difficult to articulate concretely. I myself have yet to come up with an elevator pitch that I can use at cocktail parties, networking events, or other places where they are supposed to come in handy. Expressed in terms of our inner layer, it would go something like this: "We believe in the power of Big-T Truth." And with that, I'd probably clear a room. So I, like everyone else, resort to talking about our outer layer: "We are a full-service marketing communications agency that does *blah blah* and for clients like *blah, blah,* and *blah.*" And while I'm saying this, I know that this is hardly what makes us special. Moreover, it is not enough to get us to a Level IV connection with prospects.

Thus, I've learned to accept any answer I'm given to the question about what makes a brand special, different, or distinctive. But I steadfastly adhere to the notion that meaning cannot be found in plots. It can only be found through themes.

Consider the following story:

The boy went to the store to buy some milk. When he walked in, he saw a burglar holding up the cashier. He quickly ran out of the store.

Meaningful? Compare it to this one:

The young man went to the store. When he walked in he saw a burglar holding up the cashier. Panicked, he ran as fast as he could out the front door to his car. The next day as he read the local paper's headline, "Store Cashier Shot by Burglar," he thought he should call the police to tell them what he knew. Years later, looking back on a life unfulfilled, he cannot escape why he didn't.

Both of these stories provide plots or a chain of events that occurred. But the latter provides a more important reason for the story to be told. Unlike the first story, it is more than just factual. It has what we call a *what about it*. And whether or not it's a story that hits home, it's one that we can empathize with simply because it illustrates our own potential.

The first story is similar to the type of advertising we see day in and day out: ads with an overemphasis on facts. They parade wall-to-wall features and benefits, many of them ending in *st*, as in best, fastest, or biggest, in front of viewers, and then an irrelevant theme is thrown in at the end. But more often than not, the so-called theme is more of a plot line because it implies something the brand does, as opposed to a value the brand stands for. I will discuss themes more fully in Part III when the subject becomes how to tell the brand story, once it is planned.

THE YIN AND THE YANG OF THEMES AND PLOTS

Annette Simmons, author of *The Story Factor: Inspiration, Influence, and Persuasion Through the Art of Storytelling* and one of the foremost experts on the power of story, writes: "[People] are up to their eyeballs in information. They want faith—faith in you. It is faith that moves mountains that inspires belief in you and renews hope that your ideas indeed offer what you promise." This is not to suggest that factual information, to which she refers, is unimportant. Quite the contrary. A story can't be all theme without a plot. But all plot and no theme make for a meaningless, soon-to-be-insignifiant story. As mentioned, it's a matter of finding the appropriate balance. Deciding the importance of the brand's outer layer relative to its inner layer is always a matter of judgment. However, here are some guidelines we use when facts are especially important:

1. New news: When a brand is being introduced, and especially
    when it provides a discernible and dramatic functional differ-
    ence, then it only makes sense to emphasize features and bene-
    fits. When a functional feature or benefit is new and important,
    then facts should be flaunted. Remember, in order to get to a
    Level IV connection, the lower levels have to be achieved first.

    However, do not stop here. This is not where real connections
    with the prospect are made. Keep in mind that today's news
    is tomorrow's history. If a brand is solely dependent on new
    product news to sustain it, obsolescence will take place sooner
    or later as competitive substitutes start claiming "me too."
    Furthermore, keeping the brand *new* is expensive, as additional
    outlays for R&D, packaging, advertising, operations, and a
    host of other marketing variables have to be reinvented.

    As I've said throughout this book, the ultimate goal for
    every brand should be to achieve a Level IV connection with
    the prospect. There is never a safe harbor from competitive
    activity, but once the prospect is affiliated with the brand such
    that the brand represents some important value that is shared
    by the prospect, some protection is attained.

    No matter how innovative HP becomes, an Apple user
    is relatively committed to the Apple brand. No matter how
    proven the claim that a Cleveland driver can outdistance other
    golf drivers, a Calloway user will find it hard to part with his
    Calloway. To get to Level IV, there has to always be something
    that emotionally resonates with the prospect, with or without
    new facts or product superiority claims.

2. When price is important: When price is discernibly better
    than the competition's, talk it up. However if price is all you've
    got, you will face serious problems unless you can sustain high

volume to overcome constant discounting. Price superiority is usually a better short-term tactic than a long-term strategy.

3. When risks are high: Deciding between the purchase of a Cessna or a Grumman jet will no doubt require a prospect to survey more facts than will deciding between Frito's regular or barbeque chips. Nevertheless, it's important to know that even high-risk brands can't survive on facts alone for too long. Facts become less important as brand meaning becomes something that the prospect wants to associate with.

A high-risk brand choice that we are faced with every four years is the election or reelection of our president. Political advisers know that elections are won or lost on their ability to sway voters who have little allegiance to one party or another. Numerous studies have shown that party affiliation is declining. But still, for the majority of voters, party values have more to do with their choices than does a candidate's stance on the issues. Can a Democrat be swayed to vote Republican and vice versa? It happens all the time. But what occurs most often is a vote along party lines because of the all-encompassing inner-layer values that are associated with the differing philosophies of these two parties.

THE OUTER LAYER IS THE CONFIDENCE BUILDER

Whereas defining the brand's inner layer is clearly one of the main messages of this book, knowing this does not limit the need to promote functional satisfaction that the outer layer provides. But it does put the brand's outer layer in proper perspective. The outer layer's role is not primary; it is supportive. It builds confidence in the brand so that the gate can be opened to a Level III and Level IV connection. Without confidence in how well a product will perform, there is no basis for a brand–prospect relationship to exist, no matter what the brand stands for or believes in. Brand connections are achieved to the extent that the outer layer keeps the prospect believing in the inner layer. Just as a brand will break down when the inner layer is hollow or meaningless, it will certainly perish to the extent that there is no outer support for or congruity with the brand's inner layer.

Therefore, the outer layer's role should not be taken lightly. It must consistently be the walk of the brand's talk. Especially in today's marketplace, brand confidence is becoming harder to achieve.

I have a childhood friend who, to this day, remains one of the most competitive people I have ever encountered. As a kid growing up, he was in a race to win every waking hour of the day. The most used word in his vocabulary was *betcha,* as in "betcha can't throw a football spiral

as far as I can"; "betcha my dad is smarter than your dad"; or "betcha I have more all-star baseball cards than you do." But when it came to the game of wits, he'd usually come up a little short.

One time I kiddingly exclaimed, "Betcha I can make M&M's melt in my hand." I didn't mean it as a dare, but, of course, he quickly retorted with an expected, "Betcha can't." I tried to tell him that I wasn't sporting with him. I was merely trying to make the point that those M&M ads claiming that "they melt in your mouth, not in your hand" were not completely true. He obviously bought what M&M's was selling.

"Bull!" he exclaimed. "They wouldn't be on TV if they were lying."

In stark contrast, and not too long ago, while gazing upon my two young grandkids watching a McDonald's TV commercial, the three-year-old said to the five-year-old, "Why do they say they love to make you smile? They don't make me smile."

And the five-year-old replied, "Because it's advertising, stupid."

As consumers of advertising, we have all come a long way since the early days of TV. Advertising has never been completely trusted. But over time it has significantly lost trust. We have grown to credit advertising as more false than true. As shown in a number of Gallup polls conducted in recent years, advertisers rank one notch above used-car salesmen when it comes to having high standards. And judging from my grandson, that trend isn't going to change with the next generation. My untested hypothesis is that back in the day when TV advertising was relatively new, source credibility was more readily granted. Just being big and successful enough to advertise on TV was enough to establish a Level III brand confidence connection. It's clear that much has changed. Furthermore, technology has become advertising's kryptonite, allowing people to avoid what was once forced upon them. Today, try as they might, advertisers cannot simply make claims about their outer layers and assume this will gain confidence with prospects. Source credibility is no longer freely granted. It has to be earned. And given the ubiquity of chat rooms, forums, and Internet reviews, we're getting to the point where what the advertiser claims as true or factual doesn't matter.

Not too long ago, Walmart was found to be *flogging*, or posting fake blogs. A blog ostensibly authored by a couple traveling across America in their RV and spending nights parked in Walmart parking lots turned out to be sourced by, you guessed it, Walmart. Consequently, Walmart's authenticity was called into question.

Inner and outer layer incongruities always make for attention-grabbing headlines. But it can sometimes become the subject of entire books. In his book *The Coke Machine: The Dirty Truth Behind the World's Favorite Soft Drink*, Michael Landing takes the quintessential all-American beverage to task for anti-union activities in South America, activities that have resulted in the deaths of union activists. Politicians, athletes, and celebrities provide many examples of how inner layer values can be undermined. One of the most famous cases is the Tiger Woods scandal that forced some marketers, who had paid dearly for his endorsement, to dismiss him from their payrolls. He clearly was not the Purist-Emperor we thought he was.

Hypocrisy can kill a brand. Brands must shield themselves from falsity, at all costs. Furthermore, the brand's inner layer must (not just should) be substantiated through all the brand's touch points to be perceived as true to its principles. Advertising is certainly one of the most visible touch points. But ultimately, what we often refer to as The Moment of Truth reveals itself during the interaction between customers and the people representing the brand. How a customer gets treated is the ultimate test of a brand's veracity. Too often, marketing and operations people work along different paths when it comes to service delivery. Everything the customer sees and experiences must come together as harmonious proof that the brand walks its talk.

One of the oft-used examples of outer-layer and inner-layer

alignment is exemplified by Zappos, an online shoe and clothing retailer. But they are much more than your run-of-the-mill e-tailer. Zappos has a service culture like few others in the country. I went on a tour of their headquarters in Henderson, Nevada, to experience their brand behavior for myself. What I experienced was a company that lives and breathes the belief that companies should be driven by a no-holds-barred desire to deliver happiness to both customers and employees. In an interview with *Bloomberg Businessweek*, Tony Hsieh, Zappos CEO, is quoted as saying, "Whether it's the happiness our customers receive when they get a new pair of shoes or the perfect piece of clothing, or the happiness they get when dealing with a friendly customer rep over the phone, or the happiness our employees feel about being a part of a culture that celebrates their individuality, these are all ways we bring happiness to people's lives."[3]

This belief manifests itself in a 365-day, no-questions-asked return policy, free surprise overnight shipping for most customers, and a standing offer to call about anything. And when you talk with a Zappos rep, it's likely that you'll get a handwritten thank-you card soon after your order arrives.

Zappos employees are empowered to deliver the Protector's promise of happiness. To retain people who truly want to be part of the Zappos service culture, there is a standing offer of $2,000 to anyone who decides to leave the company for any reason. And each year, Zappos publishes a *culture book* that includes statements from each and every employee on anything (uncensored) about their experience working at Zappos. Their culture book also includes pictures and descriptions of ongoing employee events that keep their happy environment alive.

Another company that actively makes certain its outer and inner layers are congruent is Cosi Restaurants. Cosi is a regional, fast-casual

---

3. Carmine Gallo, "Delivering Happiness the Zappos Way," *Bloomberg Businessweek*, May 12, 2009.

restaurant chain with locations throughout the Midwest and the East Coast. When a new employee is hired, he or she is referred to as a partner and made to feel that way. Employees are trained in Cosi's customer-centric service methods, and they learn about the unique nature of their clientele and their high regard for Cosi's service ethic. They learn that they are an extension of their brand's theme that *Life should be delicious.* Additionally, Cosi is very careful to hire only those people who can demonstrate a passion for delivering their notable service. Whether their job is greeting the customer with a genuine, "Hey, how you doin' today," baking bread to perfection, or answering mundane questions, employees are continuously supported by management, all the way to the top of the organization. Jim Hyatt, Cosi's CEO, is often seen in Cosi's restaurants walking the talk and remembering every partner's name. In addition to a constantly updated menu that appeals to the global palate of Cosi clientele, the company's service ethic embraces the idea that everything about Cosi should live up to its belief that a restaurant should provide an exploratory experience in addition to delicious food.

The value of authenticity increases as we become more apt to separate fact from fiction. As we become more sophisticated in our knowledge of things, our BS antennae have become more sensitive. Today there can be no hiding the truth about the brand underneath the cloak of what it promotes itself to be.

ACHIEVING ALIGNMENT

If one of your brand's archetypes is the Imagineer, then to support it you must be able to dramatize beauty and celebrate your imaginative products. If you see that your brand can be like the Conqueror, then ultimately you must be able to demonstrate achievement or explain how your product can help prospects achieve. The outer layer should empirically support the belief that you want prospects to associate with your brand.

When there is misalignment, as in the case of hypocrisy or irrelevance, then consumers will naturally withdraw faith in what your brand stands for. It would be totally incongruous for Harley-Davidson, the Maverick, to conduct a sweepstakes for free trips to Disney World, which archetypally is the Wizard. Likewise, it would be incongruous for Disney World to provide discount coupons for Victoria's Secret. These are extreme examples, but each time the inner and outer layers are out of sync, the inner layer is obscured and the brand-prospect link is weakened. Conversely, each time the inner layer and the outer layer mesh, the consumer's faith in the brand hero is strengthened.

So before deciding that the most promotable outer layer of your brand is speed, efficiency, or an unparalleled price/value relationship, you need to see that this benefit is only one in a series of related benefits tied to the brand's inner layer. Benefits are not one-time affairs. Rather, they should enhance other benefits that together support the brand's inner layer.

NEXT STEP

If you've identified a number of different archetypes to describe your brand, now substantiate each of them. Think of features and benefits that can now or will in the future prove the authenticity of what the brand stands for. You might be tempted to eliminate some of the archetypes at this stage if they're weak. I strongly advise you not to eliminate anything from consideration until you get to Step 3, where we'll discuss matching brand and prospect inner and outer layers.

Review

- The brand's inner layer works much like the theme or heart of a story. It is where meaning resides. The outer layer is the plot or what we sometimes refer to as the *how so* of the brand.

- The outer layer consists of the facts that support the inner layer.

- Marketers often refer to their specialness in concrete, rational terms. Describing the brand this way is like describing its body, without regard for its soul.

- Benefits should not be seen as one-time affairs. Rather they should enhance other benefits that together support the brand's inner layer.

- A story can't be all theme and no plot. But all plot and no theme make for a meaningless story. It's merely a matter of finding the appropriate balance.

- The outer layer's role is not primary; it is supportive. It builds confidence in the brand so that the gate can be opened to a Level IV brand affiliation.

- Source credibility is no longer freely granted. It has to be earned.

- Hypocrisy can kill a brand. Brands must shield themselves from falsity, at all cost.

- When there is incongruity, as in the case of hypocrisy or irrelevance, then consumers will naturally withdraw faith in what your brand stands for.

- The value of authenticity increases as we become more apt to separate fact from fiction.

CHAPTER 12

The Prospect's Layers

Great stories agree with our world view. The best stories don't teach people anything new. Instead, the best stories agree with what the audience already believes and makes the members of the audience feel smart and secure when reminded how right they were in the first place.
—*Seth Godin,* Tribes: We Need You to Lead Us

By now you are familiar with the difference between an outer layer and an inner layer. The same concept is applied to the prospect's character. Consequently, less explanation of layers is needed here. So instead of having separate chapters dedicated to each individual layer the way we discussed the brand character in chapters 8 and 9, they are combined here.

DIFFERENCES BETWEEN THE PROSPECT'S OUTER AND INNER LAYERS

A prospect's outer layer is what we often describe as the flat definition of the prospect. If a writer wants to achieve a higher degree of empathy for this character, he or she will need to round out the character by creating more depth. To do this, just as a writer would, we excavate the inner layer. Unfortunately, brand or creative briefs, if they allow for this excavation, do so in an oversimplified way in which key insights are either glossed over or ignored altogether. Taking the lead from storytellers, we spend a great deal of time fleshing out the beliefs and values that will eventually lead to a Level IV connection between the brand and the prospect (or the character and the reader, in our analogy).

The inner layer consists of relevant ideas and values that are important to the prospect. Whereas the outer layer deals with what the functional need is, the inner layer explains why that need is important. Given our goal of achieving a strong relationship with the prospect, it's vital to know what the inner layer is. Whether in stories or in real life, shared values are the foundation of strong relationships. The number and importance of shared values accounts for the difference between acquaintanceships and friendships. We all have acquaintances who share our interests in sports, music, movies, politics, bingo, or other activities. However, the people we truly bond with are those with whom we share ideas about what is truly important in life. I enjoy getting together with my buddies on weekends to swap the vicissitudes of life for the vicissitudes of the golf course. But among these buddies, my truest friends are those who have a similar outlook on life, who have similar priorities, and value other things more than a low golf handicap.

EXAMINING THE PROSPECT THROUGH LADDERING

When examining the prospect, we sometimes start with the outer layer and work back toward the inner layer. One technique that helps us do this is called laddering.

Sometimes referred to as means-end chain analysis, laddering is a research technique developed by two college professors, Thomas Reynolds and Jonathan Gutman. Essentially, laddering is used to explore both outer layer reasons and their associated inner layer beliefs for desired features and benefits. Personal interviews (called one-on-ones) are conducted to arrive at hierarchical structures of *cognitive ladders*. These ladders reflect the way we think about a given product or service.

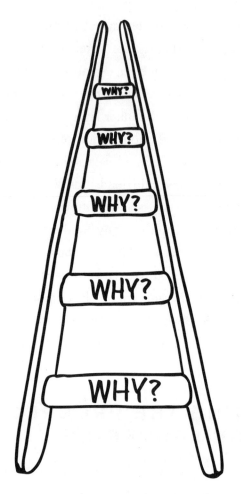

The laddering interview begins with a simple question, and then another question is asked about that response.

Interviewer: "Why x?"
Subject: "Because z."
Interviewer: "Why z?"
Subject: "Because b."
Interviewer: "Why b?"

For purposes of illustration, say we're studying a brand of laundry detergent called Bleach Bright. And one of the most important attributes cited is bleach crystals that have been shown to increase brightness 15 percent more than the leading laundry detergent can. Here's how a typical laddering interview might continue from that point:

> *Moderator: You said that bleach crystals are important when you're considering laundry detergent. Why is that?*
>
> *Respondent: Because they ensure that the whites will be white, in fact 15 percent brighter than leading laundry detergents.*
>
> *Moderator: Why is that important?*
>
> *Respondent: Because if the clothes don't come out white, they look dirty.*
>
> *Moderator: Why is that important?*
>
> *Respondent: Because I don't want my kids looking like they are wearing dirty clothes.*
>
> *Moderator: Why is that important?*
>
> *Respondent: Well, I don't want people to think that I'm the kind of mother who would let her kids wear dirty clothes.*
>
> *Moderator: Why is that important?*
>
> *Respondent: Because I'm not that kind of mother.*
>
> *Moderator: Why is it important for others to know you're not that kind of mother?*
>
> *Respondent: Because I think I should get credit for the kind of mother I really am.*
>
> *Moderator: Why is that important?*
>
> *Respondent: Recognition, I guess.*
>
> *Moderator: What do you get out of feeling recognized as a good mother?*
>
> *Respondent: It makes me feel good about myself.*

More often than not, self-esteem is the last rung of every ladder and is usually where the probing stops.

The ladder that we constructed with the aid of the prospect helps us define both of the prospect's layers. To this respondent, it is clear that white clothes are very important. This helps define the functional need that is part of this prospect's outer layer. This functional need is associated with the emotional need to feel good about her role as a mother. For her, seeing her kids in white clothes both avoids guilt and enhances recognition for being the kind of mother she thinks she should be. To another person it might be that white clothes enhance confidence. Her reasons for needing white clothes may have something to do with the notion that white, bright clothes help her to feel sure of herself while assuaging self-consciousness. In either case, laddering uncovers both problems and opportunities that a brand can address, both rationally and emotionally.

By looking at the various ladders and drawing from the demographics of respondents, we might be able to determine who the most likely prospects are, especially when the pattern of responses is consistent. On the other hand, we may find that there exist different outer and inner layer segments. When we get to Step 4 and start looking for matches between the brand and the prospect, we will be in a better position to determine which of those segments presents the best opportunity for the brand to promote or target.

OTHER TECHNIQUES USED TO DEFINE THE PROSPECT

There are two other types of techniques that can be used to get at the prospect's outer and inner layers. The first consists of a large body of projective techniques. The second consists of what some refer to as ethnographic research.

Projective Techniques

One of the drawbacks of laddering is that it asks prospects to define the why behind their behavior. Unless you are relying on a trained interviewer, it may be difficult or impossible to get a respondent to articulate his or her reasons for needing or wanting certain benefits, both functional and emotional. Projective research can be used instead. This draws from a large body of different techniques, all of which provide prompts (or stimuli) to encourage respondents to project their underlying motivations, beliefs, attitudes, or feelings onto an ambiguous situation.

Examples of projective techniques include

- Word association: The respondent says the first word that comes to mind after hearing a certain word and is asked to word-associate with competitive brands, such as Lexus, BMW, and Mercedes, to see what different words are used to describe them.

- Sentence completion: Respondents are given incomplete sentences and asked to complete them. For example, a sentence may begin with "The biggest problem I have with my dishwasher is _____, The best dishwashers are those that _____, or I wish I had a dishwasher that _____.

- Story completion: Respondents are given part of a story and are asked to complete it. For example, John and Mary are getting married. John feels that it is important to _____ because _____. Or, one of Bob's neighbors just bought a new lawn mower. Bob is somewhat envious because it is a _____ made by _____.

- Cartoon tests: Respondents are shown cartoon characters in a specific situation and with dialogue balloons. One of the balloons is empty, and the respondent is asked to fill it in. For example, a woman is shown looking at purses in a Gucci store. There's a thought bubble above her head. The respondent is asked to fill it in with what the woman might be saying to herself.

- Role playing: Respondents are asked to play the role of someone else. For example, a respondent might be asked to be an insurance salesman. It is assumed that the respondent will project his or her feelings about what to expect from insurance salesmen.

Whatever technique is used, insights can be gained about the respondents' functional and emotional needs.

Ethnographic Research

Ethnographic techniques are currently in vogue as a means to excavate both the outer and inner layer of prospects. These have roots in techniques used by anthropologists when they observe tribes, cultures, or societies. Direct observation is used to discern prospects' wants, needs, and underlying motivations.

Electrolux is a company that has benefited from ethnographic research. Instead of using marketing surveys, Electrolux regularly observes the way appliances are used in the homes of potential prospects. In one case, Electrolux was able to discern that bottled water was being purchased regularly but was using up valuable storage space. Furthermore, the assortment of refrigerators on the market that provided filtered water did so from inlets that took up too much of the refrigerators' space capacity. With this insight, Electrolux created a refrigerator that supplied filtered water and ice from a compact inlet, which also satisfied the prospect's need for tapping into the benefits of bottled water. In another case, they were able to see that households with one or two people were using large, inefficient dishwashers. Dishes were washed once or twice a week, which meant that coffee cups or other frequently used dishes weren't being cleaned every day. To meet this need, Electrolux invented a dishwasher the size of a large microwave oven that could be readily used on a daily basis.

Not only was Electrolux able to discern unmet functional needs by using enthographic research, but it also associated itself with the inner-layer value of providing relevant solutions to everyday problems. The company communicates this through its theme: "Thinking of You."[4]

Insight vs. Our Sight

Whatever research technique is employed, the objective is to gain insight into the prospect's purchase behavior in terms of both outer layer needs and inner layer values. It is important to keep in mind that the prospect's wants and needs should be accounted for through some sort of direct communication with them. It should go without saying that *our* sight, or what we think, is the reason that a given purchase behavior should be vetted before becoming something that is acted upon.

SUMMARY

At this point, you should have some idea of both the brand's and the prospect's potential inner and outer layers. In the crucial next step, we will explore ways in which we can arrive at an optimal matching of both what the brand can and should provide that will establish a strong and enduring relationship with the prospect.

---

4. "Electrolux redesigns itself," November 27, 2006, *www.businessweek.com* accessed.

Review

- Simply stated, the prospect's outer layer is found in the answer to two questions:

    ❑ What does the prospect look like?

    ❑ What is the prospect's problem that the functional advantages and benefits of the brand will solve?

- The outer layer of a prospect is what authors might refer to as a flat character.

- To achieve a higher degree of empathy, we have to convert this character into a round one.

- Whereas the outer layer deals with what the functional need is, the inner layer explains why that need is important.

- Whether in stories or in real life, shared values are the foundation of strong relationships.

- An oft-used research technique that can help identify both outer-layer functional needs and corresponding inner-layer values is a qualitative technique called laddering.

- The purpose of laddering is to arrive at underlying beliefs that explain why people behave the way they do.

- Projective techniques and ethnographic research can also be employed to arrive at insights about the prospect's buying behaviors.

CHAPTER 13

Finding the Right Match

If you will, pretend for a moment that you have been asked to write a story—not a brand story, a story story. Using story structure, you are aware that a story consists of a character dealing with an obstacle to achieve some goal. Take out the obstacle for a moment and consider the character-goal combinations you could write about. The character could be a bank robber who is setting out to conduct a major bank heist. It could be a spy who is trying to gather important government intelligence or a musician who is trying to become recognized for his or her talent. For every character you come up with, given their expected role, there will be an appropriate and logical connection between them and their goals. In the case of the bank robber, for instance, the logical goal would be to steal money, not to gather government intelligence or to gain fame for his or her musical talents.

This bank robber character/goal matchup may seem obvious, but when it comes to brand stories, matching the brand with an appropriate marketing goal is where things can go awry. Consider *Cosmopolitan* magazine when it tried to sell yogurt as an extension of the *Cosmopolitan* brand. Or Smith & Wesson—yes, the maker of guns—when they marketed the Smith & Wesson bicycle. Certainly these are extreme examples of mismatches, but there are those that seem to make some sense yet fail for less obvious reasons. Take Life Savers, the #1 brand of non-chocolate candies. They once branded a soft drink that fared well in taste tests. However, it failed miserably because prospects thought they would be drinking liquid candy. There are numerous case studies like this where a brand extension was flawed from the start because of a perceived discrepancy between the brand's expected role and its new goal.

For any brand, the ideal match is one where there is alignment between the brand's and the prospect's inner and outer layer cells. For instance, the brand's outer-layer functional solution should be perceived as a relevant fit with the prospect's outer-layer functional problem. Additionally, values and beliefs of both characters' inner layers should match up as well. Where there are mismatches, there will be problems, sometimes too difficult to overcome.

In Step 2 of the StoryBranding process, we outlined a few ways in which the brand could be described archetypally in terms of where it is now and/or where it ideally wants to be. We also considered a number of perceived functional benefits that could be associated with the brand's outer layer. In Step 3, and separate from our analysis of the brand, we looked both at and into the prospect's functional needs and motivations. We looked at possible functional needs in search of a solution, and we considered emotional needs as well. Moving into Step 4, what we have now is what I call a salad bar dilemma. Faced with different combinations and permutations between possible brand–prospect matchups, the challenge is to walk away with the best complements while avoiding a mixture of green peas with pineapples. The simplicity or complexity of this challenge is completely dependent upon the number of brand and prospect alternatives considered viable.

For the purpose of clarity, it is advisable to construct outer and inner layer combinations for each character showing outer and inner layer relationships. Once completed, look for matches between the characters. Using the Bleach Bright example that was discussed earlier, you might end up with something that looks a little like this:

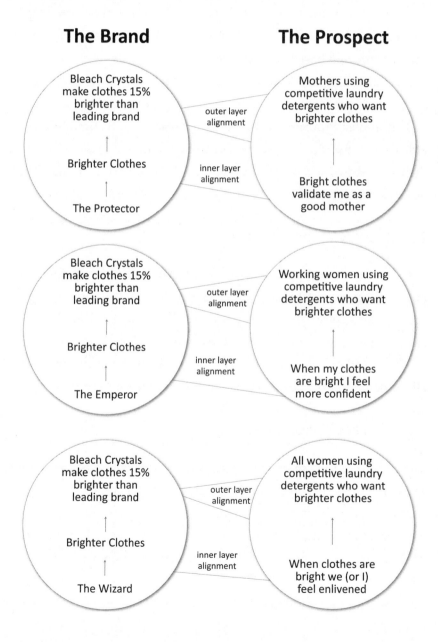

Of course, given this hypothetical situation, a number of assumptions have been made that might or might not be true. First it is assumed that the primary purchasers of laundry detergent are women who are eighteen years of age or older. It is also assumed that, while considering the prospect's inner layer and as shown in the three circles, three values were identified for three separate segments without the help of any research. It is quite possible that there are other segments and other values that could have been identified.

But assuming that, following Step 2, this is where we ended up, we see three distinct possibilities for the brand story. Let's refer to them as 1. Brand as Protector, 2. Brand as Emperor, and 3. Brand as Wizard. To arrive at the best story, and to help eliminate risk, we look at each against two criteria: (1) the quantity of the opportunity and (2) the quality of the opportunity.

The Quantity of the Opportunity

The quantity of the opportunity is nothing more than a measure of the potential size of the market. It is usually the easiest to arrive at since the answer is in numbers that can be readily obtained. Clearly in this case, for instance, the numbers are more in favor of Wizard than they are for the other two stories because we've assumed that the universe is all women, regardless of their roles as mothers or workers.

The Quality of Opportunity

The quality of the opportunity has to do with the ease of persuasion. How likely is it going to be that the outer/inner layer brand combination will fit the outer/inner layer prospect combination in each case? In some cases, it might be plain to see. My experience, however, is that in most cases some research is required, especially for instances where a major sum of money is at stake. There are a number of ways the research can be conducted and an equal number of pros and cons associated with each research technique.

In the case of Bleach Bright, and again hypothetically, let's assume that various ads were developed around each story as directed by the three concepts above.

Without getting into the methodology, following a battery of questions, we would be interested especially in three areas of investigation: (1) The respondents' indication of their *intent to purchase* the brand the way it is advertised; (2) the respondents' evaluation of *how unique* or different the brand is as advertised; (3) the respondents' evaluation of how well they identify with the brand. This is usually given with answers to a question like *is this brand for people like me?*

In general, *intent to purchase* is not always a good predictor of purchase behavior, since what we intend is not always what we do. But as a relative measure it can be very helpful, especially when differences between responses associated with each concept are dramatically different.

In the case of Bleach Bright, let's assume that scores for *intent to purchase* for the brand as Wizard were found to be dramatically lower than for the other two concepts. Further investigating why, we might see that scores for uniqueness were also much lower than for the other two concepts, as respondents told us that what is described in the Wizard ads is something they've seen or heard before. We would then eliminate the Wizard idea from consideration.

Let's further assume that the tiebreaker between the remaining two concepts was found in answers to the *something for me* question. Let's say that the brand as Emperor ads came out far ahead. Granted, the Emperor story would be sold to the smallest audience relative to the other two scenarios, but it is the concept that respondents best identify with and, as such, makes this story more appealing. The quantity of opportunity may be smaller, but the quality of opportunity is far bigger and presents fewer risks for the Emperor story, as configured in the circles.

Again, this example is oversimplified for the purposes of illustration. But it's meant to provide you with some sense of how to go about connecting the characters that you've considered in Step 2. Your analysis of both the quantity and quality of opportunity assesses both the chances of success and the chances of failure. Sometimes, the big opportunity can blind marketers to the latter.

As has been discussed, brands that are not aware of their limitations can make huge mistakes if they morph into something outside the realm of realistic possibilities. Step 3 forces one to systematically consider different strategic alternatives evaluating both risk and reward.

Review

- The brand and prospect cells have to be matched to achieve optimal results.

- A salad bar dilemma occurs when considering all the different combinations and permutations of brand and prospect matches. The challenge is to walk away with the best complements to each other, while avoiding a mixture of green peas with pineapples.

- Every brand story presents some risks. The purpose of Step 4, Connecting the Characters, is to identify opportunities while eliminating as much risk as possible.

- To do this, in Step 4, we assess both the quantity and the quality of the story's opportunity. The quantity assessment measures the size of the opportunity. The quality assessment measures the ease of persuasion.

CHAPTER 14

The Obstacles

If you can find a path with no obstacles, it probably doesn't lead anywhere.
—Frank A. Clark

The hero's path is sometimes treacherous. Happy endings are the stuff of stories where someone defeats the fiery dragon, human malevolence, the dangers of nature, or technology gone wrong. But sometimes obstacles are more psychological than physical. Stories can also show how the hero's fear, greed, denial, or other negative human dispositions can stand in the way of success.

Brands, too, must deal with obstacles both physical and psychological on their way to achieve the goal of affiliation with the prospect. We also refer to this movement to overcome these obstacles as the brand's story plot. Whereas we've discussed the composition of the characters, in order to construct the plot, now we must survey the given obstacles. Marketing classicists divide these obstacles into two camps. There are first the external obstacles, or those being exerted on the brand from

outside forces such as competition, culture, the economy, or consumer attitudes and perceptions. Then there are the internal obstacles that include things that are happening within the company that stand in the way of progress. These are usually a function of problems associated with production, distribution, and how the brand is marketed relative to the competition.

StoryBranding does not obviate the need to consider the classic barriers that most marketers will naturally consider. We did this when we described the backstory discussed in Chapter 7. But to remain true to story structure, StoryBranding reveals obstacles in a unique light, one that is related to the brand's primary goal of creating a strong and enduring relationship with the prospect.

Obstacles have levels, too.

We spoke of the staging of various connection milestones during

the brand's product life cycle. The connection between the prospect and the brand is made stronger as the prospect gains awareness of the product's function en route to an identification with the brand's belief system. To gain the desirable connection strength, we look at the individual obstacles that block or impede the brand–prospect relationship at each milestone.

THE FOUR OBSTACLES

The Level I Obstacle: No Product Function Awareness

With regard to the product function connection, the first obstacle encountered is the low-level awareness that exists for a new product that defines a new category. I provided a fictional account of the journey a man's wallet made on its way to Level IV. But we see this in real life examples all the time. This is especially prevalent in the direct response commercials we see for new inventions like the ShamWow, the Snuggie, or the Ped Egg. There's never been anything quite like these products before, so creating awareness of their primary function is the single most important feat that must be accomplished.

The Level II Obstacle: No Product Superiority Comprehension

At the next level, the product superiority connection, the obstacle is a lack of comprehension about why the brand's product is perhaps better than competitive offerings. In classic marketing-speak, this is often referred to as getting the prospect to understand the brand's unique selling proposition vis-à-vis competition. This usually takes place as the product moves from the introductory or growth stage of its life cycle.

The Level III Obstacle: Lack of Brand Confidence

At Level III, the confidence connection, the obstacle standing in the way is its opposing force: a lack of confidence in the advantage the brand claims to deliver and its claim of superiority. This could result from any number of causes, from something as simple as a lack of familiarity with the brand name to something as complex as outright disbelief. At times, the brand deals with Level II and Level III obstacles simultaneously. Level II obstacles occur when the product advantage is presented with a cogent argument and there are no preexisting conditions that impede the brand. Level III obstacles arise from either direct or indirect experiences with the brand. Some brands we will avoid regardless of their superiority claims, simply because we've had bad experiences with them in the past or have heard negative stories about them from others.

Given the influence of the Internet and social media, this obstacle can loom large for brands with product deficiencies or those that do not live up to their promises. For instance, I recently learned that I could get an iPad cover that opens up to a manual keyboard. A Level I connection was made right away because my fingers are too big to type on the iPad's touch-sensitive keyboard without hitting more than one key at a time. I then discovered there were a couple of these keypad covers on the market. One in particular was very light, in fact, much lighter than the others. This established a Level II connection because my briefcase is already an 80 lb. albatross. However, while researching this keyboard, I found a number of one-star reviews stating that the keys often get stuck. Because I couldn't get past Level III, I decided to hold off on making the purchase.

The Level IV Connection: Lack of Brand Affiliation

A failure to achieve the final connection, the prized Level IV affiliation, is usually due to the marketer's simply having ignored its importance. Many brands get stuck at Level III because they think it's the finish line. "If we can only get the prospect to see that we truly are superior, we'll win market share," goes the thinking. So R&D struggles to come up with a new and improved formula, operations develops a better way to service the customer, or distribution figures out a way to get more facings in the supermarket.

Certainly, ongoing innovation is important. In the keyboard example, I'm still hoping somebody invents a product that meets my needs. But brand marketers need to understand that any connection made at this level is ephemeral. If there is any traction gained in Level III, it is short-lived. The differentiating benefit that knocked down that Level III obstacle today will sooner or later be copied by a competitor tomorrow or become obsolete in and of itself. Dealing with Level III obstacles is like a game of Whack-a-Mole. Knock one down and another comes up.

A tactic that is often employed when all else fails to overcome the Level III obstacle is reducing the price. This, to me, is like throwing up the white flag of surrender and an indication that the brand hasn't been able to get beyond a Level III connection. Besides sacrificing margins, too much reliance on price reductions can have a deleterious effect on the brand. It's better to find ways to propel the brand into a Level IV connection than to remain stuck in Level III.

For those more enlightened brands that see the Level IV connection as something worth pursuing, failure rears its head simply because the brand is trying to associate with values and beliefs that can't be substantiated through their outer layers, as discussed in chapter 11. This is the authenticity problem we discussed earlier. Other brands seeing Level IV as the goal line find it elusive because they are trying too hard to attain it. To be achieved, identification has to be felt by the prospect.

Resonance can't be forced. Attempts to do so will be resisted and can push the brand all the way back to Level II. McDonald's was smart to abandon its "We love to make you smile" campaign before it did too much damage. For many it was hyperbolic nonsense, given the operational problems that McDonald's was facing at the time.

To get through obstacles to making a strong Level IV connection, the belief that the brand stands for must link to a belief that the prospect considers to be important. It must represent an important value the prospect readily identifies with. Additionally, it must be uniquely believable and authentically communicated through the brand's behavior or its outer layer. Once at Level IV, the brand will achieve a long-term proprietary association that is impossible for competitors to copy without looking like an also-ran.

SUCCESS BEGETS SUCCESS

Although I've presented these obstacles in sequential order, they all must be dealt with simultaneously. In the beginning, when a brand sets out to make a functional product connection, it is important to be mindful that other obstacles will show up right around the corner. I am not suggesting that brands ought to knock down all four obstacles at the same time. Brands that try to do this try to do too much at once. However, unless all possible obstacles are not considered up front, the brand will be unprepared to deal with the oncoming storm. In the worst case, the brand will be defined in terms of its product features and benefits alone. This will make it difficult to branch out with other products with the same brand name.

This is what happened to Polaroid, as it became known solely for its ability to provide instant still pictures. When it introduced a video camera, it couldn't get past the confidence obstacle because it wasn't seen as a brand that could effectively compete in the video space. Prospects questioned its ability to provide a good video camera because their association with Polaroid was relegated solely to still cameras. Xerox, a name synonymous with copier machines, ran into the same problem when it tried to introduce computers.

Apple, on the other hand, has always stood for the value of "thinking different." Consequently, this worked well in the beginning when Apple was competing with the likes of IBM and during the introduction of its MacIntosh computer. But this value is also what continues to help Apple hurdle the obstacles it faces each time it introduces a new product. Now, for instance, when Apple introduces a product like its iPhone or iPad, prospects knock down the obstacles themselves. Any product branded with the Apple name quickly gets through the first three obstacles on the way to a Level IV connection.

Apple didn't run into the same problem that Xerox ran into because from the beginning Apple stood for something much bigger than just one product. It stood for a belief that embraces everything it offers. Apple exemplifies the value of thinking ahead and envisioning where it ultimately wants to go. By deciding what it stood for, the Apple brand effectively paved the way for itself to bigger fortunes and to Level IV connections with its prospects. For the Apple loyalist customer, Apple could probably introduce an edible athletic shoe that would get instant acceptance.

Let's now turn to the story's beneficiary, the brand's prospect, who is on the other side of the obstacles.

Review

- StoryBranding reveals obstacles in a unique light, one that is related to the brand's primary goal of creating a strong and enduring relationship with the prospect.

- With regard to the product function connection, the first obstacle encountered is the low-level awareness that exists for a new product that defines a new category.

- At the product superiority connection level, the obstacle is a lack of comprehension about why the brand's product is perhaps better than competitive offerings.

- The differentiating benefit that knocked down that Level III obstacle today will sooner or later be copied by a competitor tomorrow or become obsolete in and of itself.

- For a Level IV connection to be achieved, identification has to be felt by the prospect. Resonance can't be forced. Attempts to do so will be resisted and can push the brand all the way back to Level II.

- To get through obstacles to make a strong Level IV connection, the belief that the brand stands for must link to a belief that the prospect also considers important.

- In the beginning, when a brand sets out to make a functional product connection, it is important to be mindful that other obstacles will show up right around the corner.

CHAPTER 15

The StoryBrief

The outline is 95 percent of the book. Then I sit down and write,
and that's the easy part.
—Jeffery Deaver, American mystery and crime writer

By now you are ready to execute the StoryBrief. The StoryBrief, similar to the traditional creative brief, provides a summary of strategic thought and sets up the expectations for the brand's messaging. But that's the only thing they have in common. The StoryBrief is significantly different.

As a summary of all the preceding steps in the StoryBranding process, it defines the elements of the brand's story. As such, it identifies both the brand's and prospect's inner and outer layers. Additionally, it defines the most important communication obstacles that have to be confronted for the brand to move closer to achieving a strong and enduring relationship with the prospect.

Some have argued that the typical traditional creative brief's purpose is very similar in that it asks for an identification of the prospect, how he or she thinks and feels, and what the brand has to claim in order to reinforce, change, or create its appeal. However, the difference is twofold.

First, the StoryBrief is constructed very differently as it identifies the story cells that have been analyzed and defined and together will create the brand's story.

Second, but more important, is the difference in how the questions are asked and answered. There are three parts to the StoryBrief: the brief itself, the requisite I AM statements, and the summary definition of the unique value proposition. Page one of the brief is fairly straightforward. It requires more working experience than explanation. For that reason, I have provided an example that defines each of the cells with which you are now familiar. In addition, I have provided two fictitious examples of briefs.

Page two consists of the I AM statements that round out both the brand and the prospect characters. But, as their label implies, these statements are written in the first person. They are similar to mini-autobiographical sketches of the brand story's characters. The reason for writing them in the first person will become more apparent to you as you become more familiar with I AM statements, but suffice it to say, the intent is to facilitate empathy. In this way, our understanding of the brand and the brand's prospect goes well beyond factual explanations that are the subject of traditional creative briefs. As such, the I AM statements are one of the most important, if not the most important, elements of the StoryBrief.

Page three consists of the unique selling proposition. This is the simple one-sentence or phrase that defines the value or belief that the brand is associated with. It is otherwise known as the theme line. Theme lines are not usually part of the planning process, as creative teams usually write them. In the next chapter, you'll see why we approach this task differently. Consisting of far fewer words than those found on pages one and two of the creative brief, this is often the most challenging task that is asked for in the StoryBriefing process.

Here, then, is page one of the StoryBrief format followed by two examples written for fictitious brands:

Page 1

StoryBrief for _____

1. The Backstory: What is the brand's current situation and how did it get there? What do we know about the prospect today? (Review Chapter 6 for all pertinent information to be discussed.)

   _____

   _____

   _____

2. Define the brand's inner layer: What value or important belief does the brand champion? If you used archetypal analysis, state the archetypal definition of the brand. Provide rationale.

   _____

   _____

   _____

3. Define the brand's outer layer: How is the inner layer supported by the product's (or the products') advantages and benefits? Explain why the outer layer is congruent with the inner layer.

   _____

   _____

   _____

4. What are the most important obstacles?

Given the overall objective of establishing a strong relationship with the prospect, to what extent are the following obstacles still standing in the way? Explain your answers and use this scale to evaluate: 1 = very low and 5 = very high.

a. Product Function Awareness: To what extent does the prospect know what the product's function is?

_____

_____

_____

b. Product Benefit Comprehension: To what extent does the prospect know what the product's unique functional benefits are?

_____

_____

_____

c. Brand Confidence: To what extent does the prospect feel confident that the brand can deliver its unique benefits as promised?

_____

_____

_____

d. Brand Affiliation: To what extent does the prospect have a strong relationship with the brand?

_____

_____

_____

e. Understanding that brand affiliation is the long-term goal, considering your answers from *a* through *c*, what is the most important obstacle(s) that must also be overcome in the short-term?

_____

_____

_____

5. Define the prospect's outer layer:

a. Provide all relevant and measurable attributes (e.g., age range, sex, income, family size, income, geography, etc.)

_____

_____

_____

b. What is the most important function that the prospect would want to achieve with the brand's product (or products)? Make certain that this is consistent with the brand's outer layer.

_____

_____

_____

6. Define the prospect's inner layer: What is the most important and relevant value/belief that the prospect subscribes to? Make certain this is consistent with the brand's inner layer.

_____

_____

_____

Here is an example of a StoryBrief for Bleach Bright, the fictitious brand of laundry detergent that was discussed in the previous chapter:

Page 1

StoryBrief for Bleach Bright

1. The Backstory: What is the brand's current situation and how did it get there? What do we know about the prospect today? (Review chapter 6 for all pertinent information to be discussed.)

   Bleach Bright is a new brand of laundry detergent that is manufactured by Practical Gamble. It will compete in a category that has many well-entrenched competitors (e.g., Tibe and Bliz), which are also manufactured by Practical Gamble and lead market share with 32 percent and 24 percent, respectively.

   Studies have shown that color brightness is the most desirable attribute when it comes to laundry detergent, especially among working women. From studies conducted within this segment, brightness is associated with feeling confident.

   Currently many brands are claiming that they make clothes cleaner and brighter (see competitive ads attached). Practical Gamble believes that Bleach Bright, with its unique bleach crystals, albeit cannibalistic to its existing brands, can steal share from other laundry detergent manufacturers. Many laundry detergents get clothes clean. But they do this while dulling whites and colors over time. Bleach Bright's unique bleach crystals have been tested to show that both colors and whites come out brighter than with other detergents, wash after wash. In a test of twenty washes, Bleach Bright clothes came out 15 percent brighter than those using the leading laundry detergent with bleach (measured in lumens). The reason for this is that Bleach Bright crystals are formulated to work harder on whites and colors than other bleach products do.

The brand will be introduced in three test markets (to be determined) with the same campaign.

Practical and Gamble spends a great deal on research and development and puts a lot of weight on proven performance before introducing new products. Management, being highly formalized, believes that new products must pass a number of internal financial operational and performance tests before going to market.

2. Define the brand's inner layer: What value or important belief does the brand champion? If you used archetypal analysis, state the archetypal definition of the brand. Provide rationale.

Bleach Bright will be associated with the Emperor archetype. It champions the values of confidence and accomplishment. The belief can be summed up as "looking good feels good, and feeling good about oneself is empowering."

3. Define the brand's outer layer: How is the inner layer supported by the product's (or the products') advantages and benefits? Explain why the outer layer is congruent with the inner layer.

Brighter clothes enhance confidence. Tests have shown that Bleach Bright delivers 15 percent more brightness than the next brightest detergent does.

4. What are the most important obstacles?

Given the overall objective of establishing a strong affinitive relationship with the prospect, to what extent are the following obstacles still standing in the way? Explain your answers and use this scale to evaluate: 1 = very low and 5 = very high.

a. Product Function Awareness: To what extent does the prospect know what the product's function is?

Rating: 5—Everyone knows what laundry detergent is for.

b. Product Benefit Comprehension: To what extent does the prospect know what the product's unique functional benefits are?

Rating: 1—Bleach Bright is a new product and has no consumer awareness or benefit comprehension, as yet. Specifically, there is very low comprehension of bleach crystals and their advantages.

c. Brand Confidence: To what extent does the prospect feel confident that the brand can deliver its unique benefits as promised?

Rating: 2—Because nobody is aware of the brand as yet, confidence in the brand is nonexistent. However, there is very high confidence in Practical Gamble as a manufacturer that could rub off on the brand.

d. Brand Affiliation: To what extent does the product have a strong relationship with the brand?

Rating: 1—Because the brand is nonexistent, brand affiliation has not yet been established.

e. Understanding that brand affiliation is the long-term goal, considering your answers from *a* through *c*, what is the most important obstacle(s) that must also be overcome in the short-term?

Product Benefit Comprehension. Prospect should become aware of the advantages and benefits of Bleach Bright's unique bleach crystals.

5. Define the prospect's outer layer:

a. Provide all relevant and measurable attributes (e.g., age range, sex, income, family size, income, geography, etc.).

Female, 25–49, single or married, professional, living in A and B counties throughout the United States.

b. What is the most important function that the prospect would want to achieve with the brand's product (or products). Make certain that this is consistent with the brand's outer layer.

Brighter clothes.

6. Define the prospect's inner layer: What is the most important and relevant value/belief that the prospect subscribes to? Make certain this is consistent with the brand's inner layer.

That looking good is important to the success of a working woman.

The second example is in stark contrast to the Bleach Bright example. Here, instead of a business-to-consumer brand, we have a business-to-business brand. Furthermore, we have a brand that is fairly well entrenched vs. one that is new. And we have an established product that is underperforming.

Page 1

StoryBrief for The Maverick
by National Trucks

1. The Backstory: What is the brand's current situation and how did it get there? What do we know about the prospect today?

National Truck is regarded as the leading heavy-duty long-haul truck manufacturer as measured in sales and leases to transportation companies. National's trucks are believed to have the lowest cost of operation (LCO) and the most liberal maintenance warranty of all trucks on the market.

Two years ago, National Truck decided to market a truck dedicated to the independent owner-operator. Owner-operators are highly self-reliant, rugged individualist types. They believe that working for a trucking company is a sellout.

At the time the Maverick was introduced, owner-operators regarded National Trucks as "the 18-wheel vanilla," meaning they were stripped of the functional and aesthetic appeal that owner-operators typically look for in a truck. To the owner-operator segment, National Trucks were "too corporate."

To counter this perception, the Maverick was introduced as their black sheep truck and was positioned as the Bad Boy (see competitive ads). Unlike the typical National truck, the Maverick was black on black. It also came with a unique flame decaled exterior and chrome mud flaps. It had leather seats that reclined into a queen size bed with mattress vibrator, a sixteen-speaker stereo system, a DVD player, and a small refrigerator. Except for the mattress vibrator, trucks normally sold to the owner-operator also had many of the same features, however.

Sales are currently well below projections. Surveys show that the truck competes well in price and features with the truck brands that the owner-operator is used to buying; however, the fact that it is manufactured by National poses the biggest problem.

Also, at this time, gas prices have sky-rocketed and have eaten into owner-operator profits. This fact alone has resulted in a 15 percent decline in the number of owner-operators. Many, in order to survive, have had to start working for the corporate transportation companies that they've long despised. The Maverick can show that, on average, it can save a trucker $10,000 a year in operating expenses.

2. Define the brand's inner layer: What value or important belief does the brand champion? If you used archetypal analysis, state the archetypal definition of the brand. Provide rationale.

Independence and Comfort. The Rebel (Explorer)—the Maverick keeps independent truckers from having to be fenced in working for somebody else, while allowing them the comforts they've become used to.

3. Define the brand's outer layer: How is the inner layer supported by the product's (or the products') advantages and benefits? Explain why the outer layer is congruent with the inner layer.

The Maverick is a high-performing truck, with all the comforts that the owner-operator wants, but with the LCO that owner-operators need.

4. What are the most important obstacles?

Given the overall objective of establishing a strong affinitive relationship with the prospect, to what extent are the following obstacles standing in the way? Explain your answers and use this scale to evaluate: 1 = very low and 5 = very high.

a. Product Function Awareness: To what extent does the prospect know what the product's function is?

Rating: 5

b. Product Benefit Comprehension: To what extent does the prospect know what the product's unique functional benefits are?

Rating: 4—National has a strong association with LCO among all truck drivers.

c. Brand Confidence: To what extent does the prospect feel confident that the brand can deliver its unique benefits as promised?

Rating: 2—It's a "National." Great for LCO, but the image of National comes with some negative baggage for the owner-operator.

    d. Brand Affiliation: To what extent does the product have a strong relationship with the brand?

       Rating: 1—Because it's made by National, it represents corporate values that many owner-operators are opposed to.

    e. Understanding that brand affiliation is the long-term goal, considering your answers from *a* through *c*, what is the most important obstacle(s) that must also be overcome in the short-term.

       Brand confidence and affiliation.

5. Define the prospect's outer layer:

    a. Provide all relevant and measurable attributes.

       Owner-operators who have a neutral or better disposition toward National and who place a great deal of importance on LCO.

    b. What is the most important function that the prospect would want to achieve with the brand's product (or products). Make certain that this is consistent with the brand's outer layer.

       LCO in a truck made for owner-operators.

6. Define the prospect's inner layer: What is the most important and relevant value/belief that the prospect subscribes to? Make certain this is consistent with the brand's inner layer.

    This is the segment of independent, self-reliant owner-operators who, out of necessity, have come to realize the importance of fuel efficiency. Their belief is that price should not get in the way of good business sense.

    Let's turn to page two of the StoryBrief, the I AM statements.

CHAPTER 16

I AM Statements

The great gift of human beings is that we have the power of empathy.
—Meryl Streep

Meryl Streep should know a lot about the subject of empathy. She's made it her profession. And having been nominated for more Academy Awards and Golden Globes than any other actor (sixteen and twenty-five, respectively, as of this writing), I'd say she's pretty good at what she does.

Whereas Streep was undoubtedly born with a prodigious talent; she didn't just fall out of bed one day to become one of the modern era's greatest empathizers. She traveled a long road—studying, training, and transforming her gift into a powerful skill. And along the way, she picked up a number of techniques or acting methods that help her identify with her characters in a way that allows her to embrace them.

I'm not an expert on acting—I'm just a fan. But from watching (and re-watching) countless films over a lifetime, it seems to me that there are at least two important steps for creating a character: observation and immersion.

Observation is what Dustin Hoffman did for months as he learned about savants for his role in *Rain Man*. To prepare, he met with Kim Peek, the man his character was based on, and studied numerous narrative and documentaries on savantism. But observations have to be translated into actions. And that's where immersion comes in. To become his character, Hoffman didn't just *see and do*. He went through an extensive process that involved creating specific physical gestures, experimenting with hair and wardrobe, developing a unique vocal quality, thinking about motivations and emotional responses, and probably hundreds of other things that made his performance so magical. And then, of course, he spent endless hours internalizing and practicing all of this. Ultimately, through immersion, he achieved empathy. And the line between him and the character he portrayed disappeared.

There are any number of observational techniques available to us—focus groups, surveys, specialized research methods like thematic apperception, anthropological approaches, etc. They all have their merits. But they are not enough. To achieve a higher degree of empathy, we also need immersion.

For marketers, immersion is often limited to buying or using their own and competitor's products. Certainly this is helpful in understanding the user experience. But there is still more we can do to stimulate what scientists have recently described as our brain's mirror neurons. Mirror neurons explain why we might sit on the edge of our seats during a suspense thriller, or why those of us who can admit it get choked up during certain scenes. They are also stimulated when someone describes an experience in such a way that we can feel what they felt. This is where I AM statements are particularly valuable.

From your first experience writing I AM statements, you will quickly discover that they are more than mere writing exercises. Writing

I AM statements provides a valuable immersion experience as you think and feel like the character you are describing. While writing them, I AM statements allow us to try on the individual psyches of the brand story's characters to see how they fit. And because they are written as first-person narratives, they force us to identify with the characters in ways that simple explanations cannot.

If you read chapter 1, you were briefly introduced to an example of a prospect I AM statement in the case of the Last National Bank. It is responsible for paving the way to what is now the StoryBranding process. Writing I AM statements is one of the most difficult tasks asked for by this process. In addition to writing an I AM statement for the prospect, we also write one for the brand character. For the brand, writing an I AM statement helps us to relate to the brand as a person. No matter how the brand is described, as long as it is described in the third person, a brand remains a thing. Writing about them as people imbues them with beliefs and values that humans possess. I've rarely seen a traditional creative brief that has captured the full and unique essence of the brand's character. More often than not, I'll see something like "XYZ Fast Food Company brand position: XYZ is the brand of fast food that provides real, wholesome, delicious food that our customers crave" or "ABC Car brand position: The ABC is 'first in class' as it defines what luxury and performance are all about."

Keep in mind that the goal of the brand's story is to achieve a Level IV connection, one that forms a lasting relationship with the prospect. It is hard to see how this can happen when brands are defined like this in a creative brief. People do not form relationships with fast food restaurants, cars, or any branded object's positioning. Rather, they form relationships with what the brand means to them in human terms.

If you have navigated the StoryBranding process, you have already outlined the content for the two I AM statements that have to be written. The information they will contain is found in the inner and outer layers of each character's cells. The I AM statement organizes and translates this information into language that your brand story's characters would use to describe both what they do and why they do it.

HOW TO WRITE I AM STATEMENTS

I'm going to offer a number of suggestions on how to write I AM statements. But the most important among these is to just go with it. I once heard a famous novelist who was being interviewed say that his characters write themselves. *That sounds so poetic, so prophetic, so something-an-author-might-say to sound like their talents are channeled*, I thought. But, lo and behold, while writing I AM statements, I continue to find this phenomenon to be true. Typically, I will start out with some idea of where I'm going, but more often than not, as I try to think and feel like the character, I find myself going off into places I couldn't possibly imagine from the start. So, my advice is to let the I AM statement take you where you need to go. And may the Force be with you.

I realize that letting go is easier for some than others. Nevertheless, it's an important challenge to meet head on. With practice, it comes quite naturally. For starters, I always recommend writing an I AM statement for yourself. Your own I AM statement can serve as training wheels and will help you to better understand the process. Consider some audience that you want to impress with who you are and what you stand for, maybe a prospective employer or your boss. Start with the words I AM and have at it. Your resume of accomplishments provides much of the content for your outer layer. And the beliefs and values that those accomplishments manifest make up your inner layer.

Another exercise that helps is to take a word that represents a belief or value, such as *independence* or *caring,* and write as if you were those values. Start with "I AM independence" and free-flow your ideas on what being independence feels like.

WRITING THE PROSPECT AND BRAND I AM STATEMENTS

When you're ready, you needn't be too concerned about which of the two necessary I AM statements to start with. I do favor a certain order. But however you approach writing I AM statements, the most important thing to keep in mind is that the prospect's and the brand's statements should complement each other. Once completed, the two I AM statements that you've written should provide proof that such a strong relationship has every reason to exist.

To ensure that the prospect's and brand's outer layers are consistent with each other, I usually start by writing about both of the outer layers first. To help you organize the data that you've already gathered, you can use the following steps as a guideline:

THE PROSPECT'S OUTER LAYER

1. Start with the demographics, for example, "I AM between the ages of twenty-five and thirty-four, and I am male or female, married with two kids and my income is more than $75,000." If you're familiar with what is often referred to as a persona, I AM statements are different. In a persona, you write about one person who might be within your target. I AM statements aggregate all of your prospects to provide a more generalized picture of the mass audience represented by what you've defined as the brand's prospect.

2. Speaking as the prospect, you have a functional problem that needs to be solved. Explain what the problem is and why a solution is needed. Get into the problem, experience it as your prospect would. Try to think and feel as he or she does. For example: *Having my computer go down is unacceptable. When it goes down, I'm out of business, let alone out of touch with my world. The last thing I need is someone to tell me that they'll get back to me in a week with an estimate. I need it now!*

    Err on the side of too much information. You can make it more succinct later.

3. What does successfully accomplishing the character's goal look like? How does that make you feel? Express this in an *I wish* statement. Exaggerate, if necessary, for example: *I wish I could just hit some button from inside my house to start my car on cold days.*

4. What is your character's experience with the product if it is being used currently or has been used in the past? For example: *I found the food at the Hamburger Joint to be no better than any other place that claims they make "gourmet" hamburgers.*

5. Is your character aware of your and/or competitors' brands? If so, what do you know about how it is perceived relative to competitive offerings? For example: *I think Apple computers are easier to use than PCs.*

6. Are there any thoughts your character has about your brand that are erroneous? For example: *The Mini Cooper is small. It must not be very fast.*

7. Are there any feelings that your character has about your product, or products like yours? For example: *I love my Krueger coffee machine because I don't have to wait a long time for the coffee to be made.*

THE BRAND'S OUTER LAYER

1. Start by defining what the product is by talking about features that are consistent with the prospect's needs. For example: *I am a speedy oil change for people in a hurry.*

2. Provide the rational support points for why this product can solve the prospect's stated problem. For example: *I'm the simple, well-illustrated manual for people who need fast help with their computers.*

3. Speaking as the brand, explain what success will look like for the prospect. For example: *I'm the stuff that people need to have the white teeth that make them more attractive.*

4. Talk about the advantages that you have over competitive alternatives. For example: *I'm the easiest and fastest way to get your car waxed and shined.*

5. If applicable, talk about experiences current customers have had with your product. For example: *I have been ranked highest by J.D. Powers for customer satisfaction three years in a row.*

6. Provide information that counters any misperceptions about the product that the prospect might have. For example: *I'm not a gas guzzler. I get 25 miles per gallon.*

This is what we call the *brag and boast* portion of the brands I AM statement. It is pure, unadulterated selling as we've always known it. Brag away and edit later.

From here, though, I then start writing about the inner layers. I find it easiest to start with the brand first, but often go back and forth between the brand's inner layer description and the prospect's inner layer description to ensure consistency. The writing becomes a little more challenging while navigating the inner layers of both characters. The reason for this is that you will no longer be dealing in the realm of the tangible, provable, or rational. Things get more abstract when you start to write about beliefs and values. But that essentially is what is required. Here again are some guidelines for how to describe the inner layers.

THE PROSPECT'S INNER LAYER

1. Talk about the values you subscribe to that are consistent with the brand's beliefs about what is important. Explain why these values are regarded as important. For example: *I am ethical and law-abiding and care about the environment.*

2. Make certain what you've written as your prospect's outer layer serves as proof of what you stand for. The problem you are trying

to solve should be reflected in your inner layer. For example: *I worry about my family's welfare.*

3. The most important ingredient of the inner layer is empathy. Immerse yourself in what it must like to be this person. Ladder up from what you said in the outer layer to why it is important. Explain what you mean. Don't just say "I believe it's important to look and feel my best." Explain why. Say something such as "I know that it's just human nature for people to make judgments about who I am based on the way I look. They'll never know my book by its cover, but at least they'll see they're in the right section of the library."

4. Draw on metaphors or comparisons to real things to make the intangible more concrete. For example: *I'm one of a kind in a good way. I like to think of myself as a diamond in the rough.*

THE BRAND'S INNER LAYER

1. Take from the archetypal description of your brand all information that explains what it is that you, as your brand, stand for and believe in. Go back to the archetypes and use the *sayings they might live by* as a springboard. You can even use those sayings verbatim if you like.

2. To get further inspired, I pick out a word that represents a value, say, *accomplishment*, and search the Internet for quotes, ideas, and/or thoughts about what accomplishment is all about.

3. Make certain that what you've written as your brand's outer layer serves as the proof of what you stand for. Remember, the reason the outer layer exists is because of the inner layer. It is critical that outer and inner layers be congruent.

VOICE

The primary idea behind writing I AM statements is to become the prospect and the brand. Try to write like they would talk. Don't get prosaic if your character is a plumber. Use conversational slang, jargon, even bad English if and when appropriate. Pretend you're talking instead of writing, if it helps. Go for sound, rhythm, and pace. Read it out loud a few times. Ask someone to listen to you to see if it sounds authentic. This may seem overdone or even silly at first. But how the I AM statement reads is as important as what it says. In truth, how it sounds is a very important part of what it says.

THE EDITING PROCESS

Once you've written the I AM statements, it is important to realize that these will become something that other people associated with the brand will eventually work with. Before you hand out a twelve-page, double-spaced paper on the subject, think about all of those instruction manuals that you never read and why you didn't read them. If details are important, keep them succinct. Do not be redundant. And, by all means, use paragraphs to separate thoughts.

Review

- Writing I AM statements provides a valuable immersion experience as you think and feel like the character you are describing.

- People do not form relationships with fast-food restaurants, cars, or any branded object's positioning. Rather, they form relationships with what the brand means to them in human terms.

- However you approach writing I AM statements, the most important thing to keep in mind is that the prospect's and the brand's statements should complement each other.

- Get into the prospect's problem; experience it as your prospect would. Try to think and feel as he or she does.

- The brand's outer layer is what we call the brag and boast portion of the brand's I AM statement. It is pure, unadulterated selling as we've always known it. Brag away and edit later.

- If details are important, keep them succinct.

- The purpose of the I AM statement is to evoke empathy.

- Try to write the way the prospect would talk.

- Clearly, writing I AM statements is an art form. As such, this is an exercise you will become more adept at the more you practice.

CHAPTER 17

I AM Examples

In this chapter, I've provided examples of I AM statements written by members of our staff. To protect the interests of our clients, we couldn't provide live examples, so we opted to create I AM statements for both the fictitious Bleach Bright and Maverick brands for which StoryBriefs were shown earlier. Keep in mind that these are written from assumption and conjecture. They are provided merely to offer some additional guidance.

Clearly, writing I AM statements is an art form. However, this is an exercise you will become more adept at as you practice. If your experience is anything like mine, you'll know when you nail them. Note how these I AM statements are highly consistent, with definitions provided in their respective StoryBriefs. At the same time, they provide the necessary color to enhance empathy and understanding.

I Am the Bleach Bright Prospect

Life is hectic. Balancing my day-to-day responsibilities at home and at work leaves little time for anything else. When it comes to balancing life's mundane chores—whether it's dishes, dusting, or laundry—I want to spend as little time as possible getting them done. But like everything else I do, they have to be done right.

I require products that live up to their promises. That's why I tend to buy from companies I trust. I am willing to try new things, but I must be convinced that I'm not wasting my time or money. Whether it's the cheapest or most expensive doesn't matter. I just want the best.

Professionally, I have a vision of success. And I put a lot of energy into making it happen. When I give a presentation, close a sale, or make a promise of any kind, I want my customers to believe that I'll deliver 100 percent of the time.

What my customers see of me is as important as what I say. What I wear reflects who I am. And the person I must project is someone who is bright, confident, and capable.

When I reach into my closet, I need to know that my clothes are as perfect as the day I bought them: no tears, stains, or fading. I don't have time to fix my clothes. I don't have time to redo my laundry. I don't have time to waste. Period.

I'm fairly satisfied with the detergent I've been using, and I've rarely switched. Right now, I see no reason to. It satisfactorily performs the functions I need.

I Am Bleach Bright Detergent

You've never heard of me. More importantly, you've never heard of what I can do to improve the way your clothes look.

There are any number of detergents on the market that get clothes clean. But keeping colors bright is another matter. My unique bleach crystals have been tested to show that both colors and whites come out brighter than other detergents, wash after wash. In fact, in a test of twenty washes, clothes washed using me came out 15 percent brighter than with the leading laundry detergent with bleach. The reason for this is found in my unique crystals formulated to work harder on whites and colors than other bleach products. People who buy me are like me. I believe in the power of confidence, and so do they. For my customers, good enough is never great, and they want great. For them, a lot depends on confidence. Portraying confidence says, "This is a person who is competent and can be trusted." The way a person looks won't instill confidence by itself, but looking the part goes a long way toward living the part. The self-assurance that comes from wearing clothes that are noticeably clean and bright versus dull and drabby is the most important reason I exist.

I Am the Prospect for the Maverick

When I became an operator of my own truck, it was like getting a new lease on life. No more bad routes. I could choose where I wanted to go, when, and what I wanted to haul. The days of toeing the corporate line were gone, and hopefully forever.

I got me a great rig, too. With all the comforts of home. Hell, some homes don't even have these comforts. No more vanilla trucks that say "Hey, I'm just a corporate peon." I got me a truck that says, "I don't work for the man 'cause I AM the man!" But independence don't come easy. I'm running a business now. And a lot depends on it besides my pride.

I hear too many stories about guys like me having to go back to the corporate world because they can't make it. Especially now with gas prices being what they are.

There's them that say, "So what! The prices will come down 'cause they always do." But for me, losing my independence ain't worth the gamble. The last guy standing is the one who wins in this game. And if I'm not going to be the last guy, I'm going to rank pretty close to it. Sure, I'd like to keep this cab. It's been like a member of my family. But better to be smart than broke. I'm going to stay in business for myself, no matter what it takes. And if it takes selling this rig for something that's going to help me keep me in business, then I'll do it. I just hope I don't have to give up too much of what I've become used to.

I Am the Maverick

There's no hiding the fact that I am made by National Trucks, the truck that is preferred by long-haul transportation companies. The reason for that is that my trucks consistently provide the lowest cost of operation. These days, with gas prices going up and more owner-operators going down, I don't make apologies for being who I am. In fact, I'm doing more to keep independent truckers from losing their independence than any truck on the road. Compare my numbers to anyone else's, and you'll see that I can save a trucker as much as $10,000 in operating expenses. Furthermore, while my efficiencies keep truckers truckin', I provide the same, if not better, creature comforts that can be found in trucks commonly preferred by the independent trucker. My all-black cabs come with leather seats that recline into a queen-size bed with a mattress vibrator, a sixteen-speaker stereo system, a DVD player, and a small refrigerator.

Many owner-operators became who they are by first working for corporations. They gave that up to gain freedom. Now, many of them are working for their trucks. So where's the freedom? I know that independent truckers are a proud lot. It's not easy to do what they do, and they deserve to be proud. But there's no pride in going out of business.

Now let's discuss the definition of the Brand's unique value proposition (the UVP) which is the third page of the StoryBrief.

CHAPTER 18

The Unique Value Proposition

Customers must recognize that you stand for something.
—Howard Schultz, Starbucks

The unique value proposition, or UVP, is *the* unique belief that we want both employees and prospects to associate with the brand, beyond its functional purpose. It is a brief statement, often only one sentence, that guides and directs the creation of all of the brand's marketing communications. In other words, it is damn important.

Simply put, the UVP explains the big "why" behind the brand, beyond its profit motive. A UVP might be stated as, "We believe in value of invention that is responsive, not just for invention sake," or "It's important to do things the hard way so that no stone is left unturned." As is sometimes the case, the UVP is not to be confused with its older and more familiar cousin, the USP, or unique selling proposition. As acronyms, UVP and USP may differ by just one letter, but in meaning, they are miles apart.

The USP was defined by Rosser Reeves. Reeves was an adman who worked for Ted Bates & Co., a leading advertising agency during the 1950s and the 1960s, the early days of TV advertising. By the time Reeves coined the term, TV advertising had reached adolescent wildness and was in need of reliable structure and discipline, something Reeves tried to provide in his book *Reality in Advertising:*

> Each advertisement must make a proposition to the consumer. Not just words, not just product puffery, not just show-window advertising. Each advertisement must say to each reader: "Buy this product, and you will get this specific benefit."
>
> The proposition must be one that the competition either cannot, or does not, offer. It must be unique—either a uniqueness of the brand or a claim not otherwise made in that particular field of advertising.
>
> The proposition must be so strong that it can move the mass millions (i.e., pull over new customers to your product).

On the other hand, and unlike the USP, a brand's UVP has nothing to do with describing what a brand does or how well it does it relative to competition. It extolls a belief, not a benefit. As such, it explains why the brand does what it does beyond the profit motive. It describes the cause that gives the brand a reason for being.

In story terms, the USP is most like the story's plot. The UVP is most like the story's theme. The plot of a story might be about the good guy struggling but finally prevailing to put the bad guy behind bars. In this case, the theme might be that persistence wins or that evil can't hide from virtue. The theme of any story is subject to the audience's interpretation, but it always imparts what its audience would consider a worthwhile maxim. The author's objective is to share what he or she sees as a truth, but, unlike the plot, it isn't told in the story; it's told through the story. The same can be said about UVPs. Unlike USPs that are told by the seller, UVPs are told through the selling.

The UVP does not depend on the seller's assertions. It depends on the seller's motivation.

Assertions, regardless of facts that back them up, are still subject to scrutiny, argument, and for the cynics among us, constant doubt. This is not to suggest that facts do not matter. They do. However, as has been suggested throughout this book, facts alone won't matter as much as why those facts are being delivered.

Consider the used-car salesman who might approach you with a line like, "This car has more options per dollar than any other used car on our lot." Certainly, you are not going to do a cost/benefit analysis on each car in his lot. You only have trust in him to determine if that fact is true. That trust may very well be minimized by the stigma associated with used-car salesmen. By contrast, consider the doctor who tells you that you need some important treatment. Chances are you will believe him or her. In fact, countless insurance studies have shown that the vast majority of patients do not seek out second opinions for doctor-prescribed treatments and will readily accept their doctor's assertion.

Perhaps the biggest difference between the used-car salesman and the doctor is a difference in relative source credibility. There can be no minimizing the importance of credibility. However, a fact is a fact, no matter how credible the source. As such, it can always be doubted or debated. The perceived motivation of the seller of those facts will always have a strong influence on whether or not those facts are seen as true. Enhancing perceived motivations is a function of a brand's UVP.

One strike against every brand's perceived motivation is selfish pursuit. Sellers of brands may try to convince you that they truly care about you, but we all know that how much they care is often a function of how much you are willing to pay for that care. Unlike the USP, however, the purpose of the UVP is not to directly and outwardly try to convince you of anything more than the fact that the brand stands for the same important values and beliefs that you stand for.

These beliefs are what we referred to earlier as a brand's Big-T Truth. And Big-T Truths are not talked about, they are demonstrated. They are not bragged about, they are shown.

I was once told a story about a person applying for a job who was told by the headhunter that the prospective employer was going to hire the most intelligent candidate he could find. "Be sharp," the headhunter advised. The applicant showed up for the interview and impressed all of the people he talked with that day. When everyone gathered to discuss all of the candidates that had been seen, many were taken by how intelligently this candidate answered questions he was asked. But then one of the interviewers announced, "Did you all know that he received an MBA from Harvard?" Many, upon realizing this for the first time, agreed that this particular candidate should get an offer fast and before getting one from the competition.

Imagine what might have happened had the candidate made it a point during the interview that he had an MBA from Harvard. My guess is that, at best, he may still have been offered the job, but perhaps less enthusiastically. His intelligence was demonstrated for all to see. The fact that he had an advanced degree from Harvard was the putaway shot.

THE UNIQUENESS PROBLEM

Often, two or more competitors within a category will be propelled by the same belief. The insurance category, for instance, is one where the belief in protecting others may be the brand's driving ambition.

The way protection is offered may be somewhat unique, but the value proposition itself is nothing new.

When faced with this dilemma, the best story wins. Expression and execution either add or subtract value. How well the value proposition or Big-T Truth resonates with the audience should be the ultimate test. This is perhaps more art than science, since subjectivity plays an important role. However, as a rule, when comparing executions of the same belief, we place an emphasis on resonance. This can be measured in terms of respondents' answers to questions that help gauge the extent to which the brand's Big-T Truth is identified as one's own, for example, Is this brand for people like you? or How closely do you identify with what this brand is all about and why? Although these questions do not directly reflect whether one execution is liked over another, we work from the assumption that value identification wins on all fronts.

THEME LINES VS. PLOT LINES

I'm often asked if the UVP is just another name for the campaign's theme line or tagline. The answer is both yes and no. Sometimes it might be appropriate to adopt the UVP as the brand's theme line, other times not. In the case of Bleach Bright, the UVP of "Looking confident helps one feel confident," might be a little cumbersome creatively. There are undoubtedly more memorable ways to communicate the same thought, such as *Look Confident, Feel Confidence* or something as simple as *Look as bright as you feel*. You may come up with others that do a better job, but my purpose here is to advise that you let creative expression take a backseat to the defining of the UVP first. Concentrate on the belief first, and worry about how it is stated later.

That said, and when the discussion gets to creative expressions, it is important to know the difference between what we refer to, respectively, as a theme line and a plot line.

Theme lines (or taglines) should imply the brand's belief the way a story's theme expresses the story's significance. Plot lines, on the other hand, express what the brand wants the prospect to believe. There is a big and important difference.

By virtue of the way they are stated, theme lines enlist subscription to specific human values or beliefs that are thought to be important. Drawing again from stories, a theme might be "Love makes the world go 'round," or "Crime doesn't pay." Although these aren't original, they are what we would constitute as themes simply because they imply subscription. In other words, they are intended as belief statements that resonate with people who share the belief they express. The implication is that they are important values.

Plot lines are what we typically see advertisers using. Plot lines explicate what the brand is and does from the brand's point of view. Their transparent purpose is to sell superiority. As such, they are expected and often discounted or resisted simply because they express the opinion of the seller. They have more to do with the product's USP than the brand's UVP.

For theme line examples, let's turn to some brand that is currently using them. For instance, when Apple ends its commercials with the phrase "Think Different," it is urging its audience to follow along with the notion that thinking unconventionally is important. The implication is that this belief is the guiding light that Apple follows and one that describes its intention. In effect, this theme describes what Apple stands for, while entreating subscription from those who share the belief.

Here are some other examples of theme lines that have been or are currently being used by prominent brands:

- Never Stop Exploring: North Face

- Be All That You Can Be: The Army
- Screw it! Let's Ride: Harley-Davidson
- You deserve a break today: McDonald's
- Have it your way: Burger King
- Just Do It!: Nike
- Yes we can!: Barack Obama
- A mind is a terrible thing to waste: United Negro College Fund
- Obey your thirst: Sprite
- A diamond is forever: DeBeers
- Image is everything: Canon
- Make yourself heard: Erickson

We often refer to plot lines as *brag* lines, simply because that is what they do. They express the brand's *how so?* more than its *what about it?* that we discussed in chapter 11. Plot lines are more a manifestation of the brand's opinion of itself. As such, they lack the believability and relevance of theme lines. And by themselves, they rarely make an emotional connection.

Consider the following plot lines:

- You're in good hands: State Farm Insurance
- Like a rock: Chevy Trucks
- It's the real thing: Coke
- Easy as Dell: Dell
- Your world delivered: AT&T
- Where the rubber meets the road: Firestone
- Ford has a better idea: Ford
- We bring good things to life: G.E.

One of the driving forces behind StoryBranding is that when resonance increases, resistance decreases. Theme lines increase resonance, plot lines increase resistance.

Finally, another way to think of the difference between a theme and a plot is the difference between a story and an editorial. This is not to suggest that editorials cannot effectively persuade audiences. If that were the case, whole sections of newspapers would be ignored. But stories respect our intelligence. They leave it up to their audiences to decide for themselves if their message is meaningful. Again, and sad to say, most advertising we see is tagged with plot lines. The use of theme lines, in the truest sense of what a theme line is, is generally the exception more than the rule. Implication rather than explication is one of the most powerful lessons we can take away from stories.

Review

- The unique value proposition (UVP) is the statement that sums up the unique human value associated with a given brand, such as love, freedom, independence, or creativity.

- The UVP is not to be confused with its older and more familiar cousin, the USP, or unique selling proposition.

- In story terms, the UVP is the brand's theme and the USP is the plot.

- The goal for writing a UVP is to create a simple, yet emotionally provocative statement that uniquely sums up a belief that prospects will share.

- In writing the UVP, the objective is to powerfully communicate a shared belief in a way that is charged with emotion.

- Themes should express the brand's theme the same way the story's theme expresses its significance.

- There is a discernible and highly significant difference between a theme (UVP) and a plot line (USP).

- Plot lines are more a manifestation of the brand's opinion of itself.

- Plot lines explicate what the brand is and does from the brand's point of view. Their transparent purpose is to sell superiority.

- The difference between a theme line and a plot line is the difference between a story and an editorial.

- One of the driving forces behind StoryBranding is that as resonance increases, resistance decreases.

PART III

TELLING THE STORY

PART 10

CHAPTER 19

Testing

Never stop testing, and your advertising will never stop improving.
—David Ogilvy

When budgets permit, it is highly recommended that some testing of I AM statements and alternative UVPs take place. The method we use is what we simply refer to as Resonance Development. Its name underscores its objective. The purpose of the test is to arrive at the most resonant I AM statements for both the brand and the prospect. The test utilizes qualitative and quantitative research techniques.

Using the necessary screening criteria, we hand out one or more I AM statements that have been written for both the prospect and the brand. We then ask respondents to circle the sentences that especially appeal to them, while crossing out those statements that, for one reason or another, they do not like. What remains are considered to be the neutral sentences. After this initial exercise, we go around the group

polling what was liked and disliked. Then, and only then, do we discuss the whys behind their answers.

Finally, we provide a list of different UVPs and once again ask for individuals to rate them in terms of whether or not they express a belief that is shared. We make it very clear that we are not interested in opinions about how clever or memorable the line is, so we can avoid turning the group into copywriters. In one case, we had written an I AM statement for the prospect of a fast, casual restaurant, which served a more varied menu at higher price points than traditional fast-food restaurants. In the I AM statement for the prospect, we stated the following: "I don't frequent fast-food restaurants as much as I used to."

When we collected the respondents' reactions to our I AM statements, we noticed that this statement was circled by most of the people in the focus group as being a statement that was liked. In turn, we asked respondents to tell us why they liked this statement. The responses we got suggested that fast-food employees are less service oriented. This was evidenced in statements such as "The people who work in fast-food restaurants don't really care about my satisfaction," or "Fast-food people are generally rude or careless." Furthermore we heard, "When I go to a fast, casual restaurant like (example given), people are usually more friendly and more upbeat." One person said, "I feel more pampered when I go to (example given)." This led us to revise the I AM statement to emphasize an important expectation prospects have for restaurants that categorize themselves as fast and casual.

In the I AM statement for the brand, we included the following statement: "I am mindful of the need for sandwich variety."

Many of the respondents crossed out this statement. The consensus was that being mindful was not good enough. Prospects wanted proof, so we revised the statement with specific examples that gave prospects the proof they needed.

Additionally, we typically walked away with a stronger basis for choosing one UVP statement over another. We might give prospects three or four UVP statements to choose from. Surveying the likes and the dislikes helps us to zero in on the most resonant UVPs. Furthermore, in probing with why questions, we are able to pinpoint the reasons for their choice.

A good qualitative research moderator will help arrive at the salient sentences, words, or phrases that resonate in addition to those that need to be eliminated or revised to avoid negative reactions. Again, the purpose is to develop or evolve the I AM statements and the UVP into something that works. After the interviews are completed, we are able to arrive at the optimal I AM statements and UVPs more confidently.

Review

- The purpose of the Resonance Development Test is to arrive at the most resonant I AM statements for both the brand and prospect.

- We ask respondents to circle the sentences that especially appeal to them while crossing out those statements that they do not like.

- We provide a list of different UVPs and once again ask for individuals to rate them in terms of whether or not they express a belief that is shared.

- A good qualitative research moderator will help arrive at the salient sentences, words, or phrases that resonate, as well as those that need to be eliminated or revised to avoid negative reactions.

CHAPTER 20

Big-T vs. Small-t Truth

What happens is fact, not truth. Truth is what we think about what happens.
—*Robert McKee,* Story

Once the I AM statements and the UVP are written, the messaging process begins, and all marketing communications elements are created. There's no magic formula or black box prescription to message creation. Whereas we do prefer the creative technique of storytelling, we realize it is not always practical, especially when we're working with media that require very short messages. As for other techniques, all options are always on the table.

There is, however, one principle that we adhere to no matter what creative technique we've employed. It is the same principle that is subscribed to by successful story writers that has been alluded to throughout this book. It is a belief that truth is not what is said, but what is believed.

Truth is not what is said, it is what is believed.

TRUTH IN STORIES

Stories don't create our beliefs. Rather, their themes are like magnets that find and attach themselves to beliefs that already exist. Additionally, the best stories amplify the importance of existing beliefs by charging them with emotion. Telling someone that war sucks conveys information. Showing someone how war destroys the hopes and dreams of innocent people conveys the same information with power.

Additionally, stories provide an easily digested context for truth. Logan Pearsall Smith, the American essayist, once said, "What I like in a good author is not what he says, but what he whispers." Because stories do not outwardly profess or directly tell us how to think and feel, we welcome their points of view. As we've demonstrated earlier, when resonance increases, resistance decreases. This principle has far-reaching implications for marketing communications in general, particularly when it comes to advertising.

TRUTH IN ADVERTISING

An oft-quoted statement attributed to the late Bill Bernbach, founder of Doyle Dane Bernbach, is that "the best advertising tells the truth." However, and with due respect for a man who has inspired and created so much great advertising, I've always had a hard time with this quote. I can only guess at what he meant.

The movie *Crazy People* is one of several that parodies the advertising business. It's about an advertising agency that sets out to sell honesty. In turn, it creates ads with headlines such as "Volvo. They're boxy but they're safe," or "Don't mess with AT&T. We're all you've got." For some reason, I don't think this is the truth that Bill Bernbach was referring to. So what did he mean?

Truth is an abstraction that philosophers have grappled with as far back as we can trace thought. So don't look for an accurate answer here. But whatever the definition of truth is, or could be, we all know what our individual truths are. These are what provide the engines for many, if not most, of our behaviors. Considering this, perhaps what Bernbach really meant was that the best advertising tells us something consumers believe is true for themselves. This would seem to make sense. It makes even more sense considering the effect stories have on us.

BIG-T AND SMALL-T TRUTH

Throughout this book, I have mentioned the concept of Big-T vs. small-t truth. It is not my invention. In fact, if you read only a small percentage of the storytelling references listed in the appendix, you'll run into a number of references to this concept. Different writers describe it differently. There is one description that I particularly gravitate to, however. It is from Robert McKee in his book, *Story*, considered by many to be the bible of screenwriting: "Fact, no matter how minutely observed, is truth with a small 't.' Big 'T' Truth is located behind, beyond, inside, below the surface of things, holding reality together or tearing it apart, and cannot be directly observed."

Small-t truth is objective, is either provable fact or arguable opinion. It appeals to the rational side of our brains. It typically comes at us from others who want us to know what they want us to know. Small-t truths are explicitly stated and directly communicated. In stories, they might consist of details used to describe a character or an event, for example, "The young boy felt intimidated playing chess with men three times his age," or "The circus was something everyone looked forward to each year." They are the facts that a story is built upon.

In advertising, small-t truths are explicitly stated. Small-t truths are found in statements like "The number one selling gizmo in the United States," or "MegaBright makes your teeth whiter." Besides being provable or refutable facts, small-t truths in advertising often express opinions, too: "You'll feel secure knowing you're protected by Acme Alarms," or "You'll save big during our holiday sale." It's what comprises the brand's outer layer.

On the other hand, Big-T Truths appeal to the nonrational side of our brains, where they are often colored by and linked to some emotion. Rather than coming at us, Big-T Truths come from within us. They contain our interpretations of what we're being told. We may learn small-t truths from description, but we *know* Big-T Truths from our personal perceptions and beliefs.

There is a great and instructive parallel here for creating advertising messages. If your brand advertising claims that your brand is faster, cheaper, or more long lasting, you are dealing in the realm of arguable and refutable truth. This may be necessary when trying to create a Level I or Level II connection. But it should be understood that small-t truths have major limitations. First, they have expiration dates, because competitors will soon copy them. And second, they are met with some resistance because they make the sales motive transparent.

Big-T Truths are sometimes difficult to articulate and often have to be inferred from the way we feel. "I feel scared" suggests an underlying

Big-T Truth that is triggered through identification with the source of the fear. It can be triggered by beliefs, rational or irrational, such as "airplanes are unsafe" or "the stock market is a bad place to invest money." This is one of the reasons why psychologists typically try to engage their patients in talking about their feelings. Feelings are the windows to Big-T Truths.

Big-T Truths do not always have to be communicated through words. Much of our communication is nonverbal. Production values, gestures, symbols, and other unspoken elements of an ad or commercial can often say more than words. In fact, we've been known to create highly effective commercials without words—just visuals followed by a logo and a theme. What this communicates to the audience is a respect for their intelligence—something that is often lacking in today's advertising.

This, I think, is probably one of the most important ideas to consider before putting pencil to paper or fingers to keyboards when creating advertising. Too often, we see advertisers talking more to themselves than to their audiences. They may believe that their brand makes people smile or makes them feel secure, smart, or fashionable, all the time ignoring the most important feeling people desire: the feeling of being understood. The most powerful advertising is advertising that generates a "that's me or my problem they're talking about" response. This, I believe, tops the list of important lessons that can be drawn from the art of storytelling.

Review

- Stories don't create our beliefs. Rather, their themes are like magnets that find and attach themselves to beliefs that already exist.

- This principle has far-reaching implications for marketing communications in general, particularly when it comes to advertising.

- Whatever the definition of truth is, or could be, we all know what our individual truths are.

- Small-t truth typically comes at us from others who want us to know what they want us to know.

- Big-T Truths appeal to the nonrational side of our brains where they are often colored by and linked to some emotion. Rather than coming at us, Big-T Truths come from within us.

- The most powerful advertising is advertising that generates a "that's me or my problem they're talking about" response.

CHAPTER 21

The Care and Feeding of the Creative Animal

*If your actions inspire others to dream more, learn more,
and become more, you are a leader.*
—John Quincy Adams

I've spent my entire career on the agency side of the marketing communications business. A great deal has changed during these past thirty-plus years. But one thing, unfortunately, remains the same. It has to do with the way creative talent is generally utilized by clients and agency personnel alike.

There are a lot of people responsible for the success of a brand. But few have as much to do with the way a brand is projected to consumers as the creative team in charge of a brand's message. And when it comes to that task, there is a lot on the line. Perhaps this explains, in part, why creative people are sometimes micromanaged by fearful

clients and account people with direction that includes everything from the rewritten headlines to copy and/or a drawn layout. Unfortunately this happens often enough that creatives have coined the phrase *being wristed* to describe how this behavior makes them feel.

I am not suggesting that those who are referred to as the creatives are the only creative people associated with a brand. They are most definitely not. However, these are people who spend the greater part of their day creating word and picture combinations that communicate to consumers. Many have a great deal of experience and are constantly on the lookout for ways to up their messaging skills. If you have any doubts about that, sit through a TV show with a writer or an art director. The best among them are not people who will readily fast forward through commercials. Instead they watch while asking themselves, "How could I have done it better?"

Creatives are not infallible. But they do have experienced judgment that is the result of their specialization. The best way to take advantage of that specialization is to inspire their output rather than dictate it. In my experience, I have found that the best creative people are synthesizers. They are like super-absorbent sponges taking in tons of information from their senses. Then, after combining that information with the storehouse of information already packed away in their heads, *presto changeo*: new ways of seeing things are born. How creatives arrive at good ideas is a function of many uncontrollable factors. But as the people in charge of planning the brand story, there is one factor that we can and must control: the information we give them from the start.

A current that has run through this book is the notion that creatives must be inspired to do their best work. Inspiration goes beyond giving the facts. It includes a nonrational, felt-more-than-explicated engagement with the reasons behind the facts. The best creative direction includes involvement and immersion—something a data dump can't provide. Creatives do their best work when their senses are enlivened, when they see and feel for themselves what the prospect sees and feels, and when the brand is something they experience, the same way they would experience another human being.

Yes, certain objectives must be accomplished, but too often in an effort to make sure that the creative output achieves its goal, emphasis is placed on what should or shouldn't be considered or, worse yet, said. Instead, when we provide creative input, we do it with more emphasis given to what will inspire original thinking than contain or constrict it. For some this is uncomfortable, as a certain amount of control has to be given up. Fear of not getting what is needed creeps into creative briefs with statements such as "the tonality of the message should be humorous," or "ads should state that Brand X is durable and lasts a long time." But, as we've seen time and time again, the best thinking is usually the product of freedom. I AM statements allow that freedom, as they favor interpretive over regulated thinking. They do not provide the do's and don'ts. Rather they leave it up to the creative team to naturally arrive at what's most important to be communicated as well as how it can best be communicated.

Review

- There are a lot of people responsible for the success of a brand. But few have as much to do with the way a brand is projected to consumers as the creative team in charge of a brand's message.

- Many creatives have a great deal of experience and are constantly on the lookout for ways to up their messaging skills.

- Creatives do their best work when their senses are enlivened, when they see and feel for themselves what the prospect sees and feels, and when the brand is something they experience, the same way they would experience another human being.

- As the people in charge of planning the brand story, there is one factor that we can and must control: the information we give them from the start.

CHAPTER 22

Sell the Truth

Storytelling reveals meaning without committing the error of defining it.
—Hannah Arendt, political theorist

The two words at the end of every story tell the audience where the story stops. These two words signal the time when the author's voice stops and our inner voice begins. For that reason, *The End* is more of a beginning. It invites the audience to put the story into their own personal perspective, deciding on its relevance and personal meaning.

This is The End to my story. Having presented the case for approaching brands as stories, it is now up to you to decide on how that can be done. For some, StoryBranding is a radical departure from traditional marketing communication planning processes. For others, it is a natural extension of what has gone before it. My hope is that, at the very least, it has provided a new perspective that can help marketing communicators draw on one of the oldest persuasive tools known to mankind.

I've often wondered why, after thirty years in the advertising and marketing business, I discovered the benefit of seeing brands as stories. Perhaps it is because I've been too hard-headed to see something that was staring me in the face just waiting to be discovered. Perhaps it is because I was blinded by too many rules that led me astray from the importance of simply Selling the Truth. I'm not sure, nor do I think I'll ever be sure.

But this much I do know. Seeing brands as stories has opened me up to following new routes to similar destinations and new destinations that could not have been found otherwise. I've come to appreciate what brands really are beyond the typical textbook definitions.

It is only fitting that I end this book on StoryBranding with a story. What follows is a story that I adapted from a Hasidic folk tale, and one that best summarizes one of the most important lessons I've learned about Selling the Truth.

The Story About Small-t and Big-T Truth

Small-t truth walked into a village. The local inhabitants started cursing at him. Spewing epithets, they chased him out of the village.

He walked, lonely and sad, down the empty road, until he reached the next town. He was still hoping to find someone who would be happy to see him, who would embrace him with open arms.

And once again, the townsfolk yelled at him. "LEAVE US BE! Go back to where you came from!" they shouted.

Not understanding why they were so upset, he continued his journey. Arriving at the third town in the middle of the night, he was hoping that dawn would find the townsfolk happy to see him and hear what he had to say. But as soon as the townsfolk's eyes lit upon him, they ran to their homes and came back throwing garbage. "GET OUT OF HERE! We don't want to hear what you're telling us!" they bellowed.

Small-t truth ran off into the woods crying. After cleaning off the garbage, he heard sounds coming from the edge of the woods. As he approached the sound, he could hear laughter and applause.

He saw that Big-T Truth had come into town. And the townsfolk were thrilled. They brought out fresh meats and soups and pies and pastries and offered them all to Big-T Truth, who smiled and relished their love and appreciation.

Later that evening, and just before going to sleep, Big-T could hear someone crying in the woods. He followed his curiosity into the woods only to discover a smaller version of himself sobbing. "Are you okay?" he asked.

Small-t truth said, "No, I'm not. I've been to three towns and the townsfolk have all treated me badly. I don't know why. I just want to be appreciated like you!"

Sizing up the situation, Big-T Truth replied, "Of course they all reject you. You're representing your truth. The townsfolk don't want your truth. They want their own. You're trying too hard to convince them of your truth. All you need to do is show them what they already believe is True. They will never listen to you unless they can identify with you."

So Big-T Truth gave small-t truth some new clothing. "Here," he said, "wrap yourself in their Truth; it will help you resonate with them. And less I promise you, they will see you differently."

The next day small-t truth walked into the village in his new clothing. And lo and behold, the townspeople greeted him with love and appreciation, for Truth's clothing is indeed a beautiful thing to behold.

"You were right, Big-T Truth!" small-t truth shouted. "How can I ever thank you?"

"Travel with me," Big-T Truth said. "Now that you know what Truth really is, we shall be great partners."

So from that day forward they traveled together. And they were accepted and loved everywhere they went.

And that's the way it was, the way it is, and the way it shall always be.

The End.

Good luck and good StoryBranding.

truth vs. TRUTH

References and Suggested Reading

Bedbury, Scott, and Stephen Fenichell. *A New Brand World: 8 Principles for Achieving Brand Leadership in the 21st Century*. New York: Viking, 2002.

Blanding, Michael. *The Coke Machine: The Dirty Truth Behind the World's Favorite Soft Drink*. New York: Avery, 2010.

Denning, Stephen. *The Springboard: How Storytelling Ignites Action in Knowledge-Era Organizations*. Boston: Butterworth-Heinemann, 2001.

Ferrell, William K. *Literature and Film as Modern Mythology*. Praeger Paperback, 2000.

Gabriel, Yiannis. *Myths, Stories, and Organizations: Premodern Narratives for Our Times*. Oxford, New York: Oxford University Press, 2004.

Godin, Seth. *All Marketers Are Liars: The Power of Telling Authentic Stories in a Low-Trust World*. New York: Portfolio, 2005.

Godin, Seth. *Tribes: We Need You to Lead Us*. Brilliance Audio on MP3-CD, 2008.

Hanlon, Patrick. *Primal Branding: Create Zealots for Your Brand, Your Company, and Your Future*. New York: Free Press, 2006.

Haven, Kendall F. *Story Proof: The Science Behind the Startling Power of Story*. Westport, CT: Libraries Unlimited, 2007.

King, Stephen. *On Writing: A Memoir of the Craft*. New York: Scribners, 2010.

Lakhani, Dave. *Persuasion: The Art of Getting What you Want*. Wiley, 2005.

Lipman, Doug. *Improving Your Storytelling: Beyond the Basics for All Who Tell Stories in Work Or Play*. Little Rock, AR: August House, 1999.

Margolis, Michael. *Believe Me: Why Your Vision, Brand, and Leadership Need a Bigger Story*. Get Storied Press, 2009

Mark, Margaret, and Carol Pearson. *The Hero and the Outlaw: Building Extraordinary Brands Through the Power of Archetypes*. New York: McGraw-Hill, 2001.

Mathews, Ryan, and Watts Wacker. *What's Your Story?: Storytelling to Move Markets, Audiences, People, and Brands*. Upper Saddle River, NJ: FT Press, 2008.

Maxwell, Richard, and Robert Dickman. *The Elements of Persuasion: Use Storytelling to Pitch Better, Sell Faster & Win More Business*. 1st ed. ed. New York: Collins, 2007.

McKee, Robert. *Story: Substance, Structure, Style, and the Principles of Screenwriting*. 1st ed. New York: ReganBooks, 1997.

Naisbitt, John. *Megatrends: Ten New Directions Transforming Our Lives*. New York: Warner Books, 1982.

Pink, Daniel H. *A Whole New Mind: Why Right-Brainers Will Rule the Future*. Riverhead Trade (Paperbacks), 2006.

Porter, Michael E. *On Competition*. Updated and expanded ed. Boston, MA: Harvard Business School Pub., 2008.

Reeves, Rosser. *Reality in Advertising* [1st Borzoi ed.]. New York: Knopf, 1961.

Simmons, Annette. *The Story Factor: Inspiration, Influence, and Persuasion Through the Art of Storytelling*. New York: Basic Books, 2001.

Simmons, Annette. *Whoever Tells the Best Story Wins: How to Use Your Own Stories to Communicate with Power and Impact*. New York: Amacom, 2007.

Smith, Logan Pearsall. *Afterthoughts*. Constable, 1931.

Vincent, Laurence. *Legendary Brands: Unleashing the Power of Storytelling to Create a Winning Marketing Strategy*. Chicago: Dearborn Trade Pub., 2002.

About the Author

Jim Signorelli has always had a passion for advertising. His favorite activity in grade school was "show and tell." As a paperboy, he would add subscribers by copy testing leaflets, where he found that the tagline "If you buy from me, I promise not to throw your paper in the bushes," outsold "You need the news, I need the money. Let's strike a deal."

After receiving both a B.A. and an M.A. in advertising from Michigan State University, Jim started his adult career in nearby Chicago. He later worked in New York, Los Angeles, and Baltimore amassing experience on a wide variety of major accounts such as Citibank, Kraft Foods, Burger King, General Electric, Toshiba, Arby's, and many others.

In 1999 he started his own agency in Chicago that today goes by the name ESW Partners. The agency has been named to the Inc. 5000 list of fastest-growing independent companies in the U.S. for three years straight.

Around 2006, Jim became interested in storytelling, stumbling upon the notion that the way stories work provides significant power to enhance brand strategies and advertising. This discovery was the inspiration for *StoryBranding*.

When he's not running—or hiding from running—an advertising agency, Jim is an avid golfer, tennis player, drummer, and Pez dispenser collector. He is also the very avid husband of his wife, Joan. They live, play, and share lots of stories with each other at home in Evanston, Illinois.